Grammar

Quick, Simple Solutions to Problems Like "Do I Say Him and Me, or He and I?"

By Carolyn Henderson

Copyright 2012 by Carolyn Henderson

All Rights Reserved

Also by Carolyn Henderson

Life Is a Gift (e-book)

The Jane Austen Driving School (e-book)

Coming in 2013

Punctuation Problems -- Let's Solve Them

Contents

Introduction 1
WORDS THAT SOUND THE SAME BUT ARE
SPELLED (AND USED) DIFFERENTLY 6
It's and Its 9
You're and Your 12
They're, Their, There.. 14
Well and Will... 19
Then and Than 23
Two, To, Too 27
Are and Our 34
WRITING MECHANICS 36
Who, That, and Which.. 37
Who and Whom 41
Formal versus Informal Writing 46
Varying Your Sentence Structure.............................. 51
What Is a Sentence?.. 56
Paragraphs Matter.. 68
Capitalize the Word "I" 75
How Do You Capitalize a Title? 76
General Rules for Capitalizing 79
Is It a Sin to End a Sentence with a Preposition? 82
Is It a Sin to Begin a Sentence with a Conjunction? 86
Overuse of Would, Can, and Could........................... 88
Must, Should, and Ought 90

Passive Construction -- a Powerful Tool 92

THINGS WE DIDN'T WORRY ABOUT 150 YEARS AGO 97

"Moving Forward with Intention" and Other Non-Communicative Phrases 99

Gender Issues 101

Do I Use Mrs., Miss, or Ms.? 107

Online Writing and Key Words (Search Engine Optimization) 110

Online Writing – Simple Graphic Design Ideas 114

Blogging 116

How to Write a Decent E-mail 118

How to Write a Thank You Note 127

Do I Say "Him and Me" or "He and I"? 130

Thank You 136

To My Mother,

The daughter of Polish immigrants who never, ever let me get away with saying, "Her and me are going to the movies."

Thanks, Mom. This is your legacy.

Introduction

This is sort of a grammar book.

I say "sort of" because it's more important to me that you get your question answered quickly and get back to your writing, than that you be assaulted by restrictive clauses, prepositional phrases, and the accusative versus the subjective case.

For this reason, I have done my best to keep grammar terms to a minimum, and to explain them in such a way that you don't have to be an avid diagrammer of sentences in order to grasp what we're talking about.

In other words, this is a book for people who want to write – and sound reasonably intelligent doing so – as opposed to study grammar. Most of us manage to speak with some degree of educated awareness, and as long as you *don't make no practice to use no double negatives* or participate in a similar butchering of our verbal heritage, you should be able to answer many of your dilemmas by simply asking yourself,

"Does it sound right?"

The more you read – well written, decently edited material – and the more you surround yourself by people who speak conventionally respectable English, the more success you will have in expressing yourself verbally.

The purpose of grammar, punctuation, and spelling is not to make people feel dumb because they don't know what a dangling participle is, much less whether or not they want to use one. Nor is it to keep English teachers employed. Grammar, punctuation, and spelling are tools that enable us to understand one another better, because there is a consistency of how things are done. Like this sentence, purportedly set before a group of students by a nameless English teacher, who told them to punctuate it:

Woman without her man is nothing.

As the story goes, most of the men wrote this:

Woman, without her man, is nothing.

While most of the women wrote this:

Woman: without her, man is nothing.

Whether or not the demographic breakdown of this is true, the sentence illustrates a point: where you put punctuation is important, and something as small as a comma can change the entire meaning of a sentence.

Spelling, likewise, is more useful than it is frustrating:

Y cant we al spel stuf foneticly? It wood b ezer.

While this plaintive question seems logical, in a perfect world where phonetic spelling ruled, we would still stumble upon differences, necessitating rules. The aforementioned sentence could also be spelled, phonetically, like this:

Wi kant wee ol spel stuf fonetukle? It wud be eseur.

Grammar, while it seems picky and pedantic (and it is, sometimes; grammarians are as renowned for arguing with each other as they are pointing out the syntactic foibles of others), serves a similar function – it provides a sense of continuity and order that enables us to collectively understand certain rules, with the ultimate goal of making communication easier.

I have chosen to focus on issues that come up again and again, in the interests of keeping things short, sweet, and easy to understand, and I'm sure that I've missed something, somewhere. If that's the case, and there is a writing question that repeatedly assaults you, please let me know. You can reach me via the Contact Form at Steve Henderson Fine Art online (www.stevehendersonfineart.com) , which I co-own with my husband, Steve Henderson, the one responsible for the fine art.

I have loosely ordered this book into sections:

Words That Sound the Same but Are Spelled (and Used) Differently – when you mention the concept of "grammar issues," these particular problem words come hurling toward you from all directions. They are generally accompanied by groans of mental anguish.

Writing Mechanics – a random assortment of writing issues, ranging from abstract concepts such as how to vary your sentence structure to the more concrete, as in whether or not you will get in trouble for ending your sentences with a preposition.

Things We Didn't Worry about 150 Years Ago -- blogging, e-mailing, offending people by calling them Mrs. instead of Ms. We'll look at contemporary writing issues that Jane Austen didn't have to dream of worrying about.

The Him and Me and He and I Dilemma – This deserves to be in a category all its own.

You probably noticed that there's nothing about punctuation in the table of contents, for the excellent reason that this is a separate book of its own. When I've got it done, I'll do my best to let you know. (If you follow us on the Steve Henderson Fine Art Facebook or sign up for our free weekly e-mail newsletter, *Start Your Week with Steve* at www.SteveHendersonFineArt.com, you won't miss out. I post everything of interest in these two places.)

Again, the purpose of this book is to answer your question as quickly as possible without inundating ourselves in the density of grammar. Feel free to jump through chapters and read what interests or perplexes you; if I feel that you need to read one chapter before understanding another one, I'll let you know.

Keep this in mind:

It is possible to write well without knowing the nuances of grammar.

It is also possible to know all of the nuances of grammar and be unable to write well.

Of the two, I'll take Option 1.

With that in mind, let's get started.

WORDS THAT SOUND THE SAME BUT ARE SPELLED (AND USED) DIFFERENTLY

The first section of this book deals with words that we frequently confuse because, even though they mean something very specific, they sound pretty much the same when we say them aloud, and they don't look that different when we write them out.

Officially, these are called "homonyms," with the prefix "homo" meaning "same," and "nyms" meaning "names" – same names. Unofficially, they're irritating.

Learning how to use these words correctly involves two steps:

1) **Identifying the differences in usage and meaning between the words** – if you don't know there's a problem, you can't solve it – and

2) **Memorizing which word does what.** There is no shortcut to this. While I try to provide a ditty here and there, the ultimate driving it into your brain – and your default way of thinking – will take concentrated practice, either by memorizing the ditty, or focusing on the word itself and memorizing its function.

Years ago, I could never remember how to spell the word "license," which I varied in spelling as "license," "licence," "lisence," and "lisense." They all looked right to me, and since this was long before spell-check and its squiggly red underlines, my computer wasn't helping me out.

So I focused on the word – spelling it aloud, writing it down, staring at it, spelling it aloud again until finally, "license" looked and felt right. Admittedly, however, I still stop and consciously consider the word – 30 years later. It's simply a difficult word for me.

You have your own difficult words and phrases – which is probably why you're reading this book. I hope to be a part in the successful conquering of your personal word and phrase challenges, but I can't do the hardest part: practicing. Pick one word, one problem, and focus on it.

How long will this take?

As long as it takes.

In the back of our minds we all hear the voices that proclaim, "Facts are not stored in your long-term memory until they have been studied three times. Or seven. Or 15. Or 23."

There is no official number because there is no official brain. The only certainty is that truly learning something takes time and practice, and how much time and practice depends upon the individual. You are not dumber than everyone else; your brain is not fuzzier than everyone else's; you are not inferior; and the case is not hopeless.

Give yourself a break by recognizing that you are an individual, with strengths in certain areas and weaknesses in others, and what works for someone else will not work the same for you. There's no use spending energy – which you'll need to grasp the concepts you're having trouble with – berating yourself.

It's and Its

Life's in the small things, they say, and punctuation marks, like the apostrophe in the word, "It's," are small indeed. But that doesn't mean that they're not important.

When I was younger, and we wrote more essays and letters and memos and assignments by hand, you could eclipse this problem by hovering the apostrophe somewhere over the word and making the symbol really small -- so that it could either be an apostrophe, or an accidental splotch from the pen. Not so on the computer.

But it's really not complicated when you realize that one of the purposes of the apostrophe is to tell us that there used to be letters in that spot, and they're not anymore. In other words, the word "It's" that we're talking about is an abbreviation:

It's means, "It is."

We dropped the second "i," shoved the "s" up against the "t," and inserted the apostrophe -- ' -- to tell the reader that there used to be a letter there, in this case, the second "i."

That's the only time you use "it's" with an apostrophe -- to say "it is" in abbreviated form. You use "its," without the apostrophe, for everything else -- generally, to describe possession:

I hate that dog -- I don't know what its problem is.

That book has all its pages ripped out.

The vacuum? Its major problem is that it's (it is) not working.

Here's where the confusion comes in:

Apostrophes are baffling things, and most of the time, we use them to show possession, as in "The dog's tail," or "The sewing machine's needle." These sound so much more natural than "The tail of the dog," or "The needle of the sewing machine," but that's basically what a *possessive apostrophe*, which is what we call the thing when it's telling us that something belongs to somebody else, is doing.

Suffice it to say that many people vaguely know that they're supposed to use an apostrophe when they want to describe something as belonging to someone or something (possession), and when they use its in the manner of the three sample sentences above, they feel this urgency to add the apostrophe:

I hate that dog -- I don't know what it's problem is.

No. NO. NO!

Remember that "it's" with an apostrophe ALWAYS means "it is, " and you wouldn't say,

I hate that dog -- I don't know what it is problem is, would you?

Then don't use the apostrophe. To put it in more official grammatical terms, you don't use apostrophes to show possession when you're using what we call a *pronoun*, as in its, his, her, your, their, or our.

To encapsulate:

"It's" always means "it is." If you can replace the word "It's" in your sentence with "it is," then use the apostrophe. Otherwise, use "its", without the apostrophe.

And now for your valid question: **how can I remember which one is which?**

Look at the apostrophe in "it's."

It's kind of tiny, isn't it? It almost looks like the leftover dot from the "i" that used to be there, doesn't it? Well, let's pretend that it is indeed that dot, and all that is left from the "i" of "is" that used to be there is that little apostrophe. This is a reminder to you that the apostrophe is used to show an abbreviation – like "it's" for "it is" -- alerting us that there used to be a letter there that no longer is – kind of like the shoe from the Wicked Witch of the East, peeking out from underneath the house, in the 1939 movie, *The Wizard of Oz*, alerting us that there used to be a full-fledged witch flying around.

You're and Your

Once you've got "it's" and "its" down, it's a small step to conquer "your" and "you're," because the principle is the same:

"You're" is an abbreviation that means "You are," and the apostrophe is placed between the "u" and the "r" to tell the reader that there used to be a letter there, in this case the "a" of "are."

Use "you're," with the apostrophe, in any sentence where you can replace the one word with the two words, "you are."

You're (you are) odd.

You're (you are) going to be late to your meeting.

In all other cases, use your:

That's your problem, not mine.

Is this your coffee?

If you're (you are) not eating your doughnut, may I have it?

Let's see. Is there some ditty or irritating rhyme that we can use to remember this?

You're. Little tiny line. You swine. You ate the "a."

Such hate when you abbreviate. You ate the "a."

Okay, so this isn't Shakespeare, and by all means feel free to make up your own dumb ditty to remind yourself of the difference between these two words.

I have found that, in making up dumb ditties for mnemonic purposes, the dumber they are, the easier they are to remember, which is the purpose behind why we create them in the first place.

They're, Their, There

If you've got It's and Its, and You're and Your under your belt, you shouldn't have too much trouble with They're, Their, and There, even though there's an extra word tossed in.

Let's start with the easiest first: They're.

It means "they are."

That's it for this one, and the only time you use "they're" with the apostrophe is when you want to say "they are."

They're (they are) going to the store.

I'm not sure if they're (they are) coming.

It's frustrating because they're (they are) always late.

"Their" is a *possessive pronoun* along the lines of My, Your, His, Her, or Our; it is used in front of a noun – a person, place, or thing – to tell us that the object in question belongs to a particular set of people:

Where is their house?

The easiest way to figure out whether or not you should be using Their in the sentence is to replace it with His or Her and see if it still makes sense:

Where is their (his/her) house?

What is their (his/her) opinion on the matter?

With this in mind, look at these misuses of "Their" and see how replacing His or Her makes the error more obvious:

Incorrect: *Their (His/Her) are six cats in the kitchen.* (There are six cats in the kitchen.)

Incorrect: *The book is on the table over their (his/her).* (The book is on the table over there.)

Incorrect: *Their (His/Her) going to be late for dinner.* (They're – They are – going to be late for dinner.)

If the whole his/her thing makes sense, but you can't remember the spelling of "their," maybe this ditty will help:

Mom and Dad aren't fair.

They say I have to share.

I'm not their only heir.

Okay, I know it's long, but it is catchy and it rhymes and everything The main point, however, is that the word "heir," as in "their only heir," is spelled like "their" without the "t." So when you're talking about "their heir," or "their bear," or "their glare," you use the "their" that's spelled like "heir."

Once you recognize and understand that "Their" and "They're" have pretty specific, limited uses, you're close to the end. Basically, everything else uses the word "There."

You don't need to worry that There is sometimes called a *demonstrative adverb*, signifying place (*He's over there*), or other times a controversially defined pronoun (*There are a lot of problems with this paper*). All you need to know is that, if you're not trying to say "they are" (They're), and you can't reasonably replace the word with "his/her" (Their), then you probably need the word There.

If you can answer the question Where? (which is spelled just like "there" except it begins with a "w" instead of a "t") you're probably looking at the word There:

I see him over where? I see him over there.

Put the book where? Put the book there.

Also, you'll use "there" in "there is," "there are," constructions – if you speak Spanish, these constructions are similar to "hay" as in "*Hay tres gatos en la sala*," – in French, it's "il y a" – *"il y a trois chats en la sale"*:

There are three cats in the room.

There is a marshmallow on top of my cookie.

"There" wears a lot of hats, which is why people misuse it so much.

Want to practice?

1) There/Their/They're going to be late if they don't get here soon.

2) I don't understand there/their/they're negative attitude.

3) There/Their/They're are too many cats in this kitchen.

4) Will you be there/their/they're by 3 p.m.?

5) There/Their/They're books are on the coffee table.

6) There/Their/They're always leaving there/their/they're books over there/their/they're on the bathroom floor.

Answers:

1) They're (They are) going to be late if they don't get here soon.

2) I don't understand their (his/her) negative attitude.

3) There are too many cats in the kitchen. (Neither They are or His/Her makes sense)

4) Will you be there (where?) by 3 p.m.?

5) Their (His/Her) books are on the coffee table.

6) They're (They are) always leaving their (his/her) books over there (where?) on the bathroom floor.

Well and Will

One of the biggest hurdles about understanding these two words is grasping that they are pronounced differently:

"Well" rhymes with "Swell" -- and generally, when you're feeling swell, you're doing well.

"Will" rhymes with "Swill," a repulsive watery gruel that I have no intention of eating for dinner tonight.

"Well" is never used as a *verb* -- (a verb is an action word describing something that you are doing) -- so you NEVER say:

They well eat something. Incorrect!

I well see you tomorrow. No!

He well be by this afternoon after 2. Argghh!

If you can't grasp what a verb is, then think of it this way: If you can use "won't" in the sentence, then you can use "will," only for the opposite meaning:

He won't be by in the morning. He will be by in the morning.

They won't eat turkey. They will eat turkey.

Won't he read that book? Will he read that book?

If you can use "won't," you can use "will," not "well." Swell.

"Will," with an "i," puts whatever we're doing into the future:

I will eat (later).

You will see him tomorrow.

Will we be in time to catch the bus?

In the three sentences above, "eat," "see," and "be," are all verbs, describing something that they, I, or he are doing. We add the word "will,' with an "i," to put that something they're doing into the future.

Use "will" any time you are talking about something that you, your mother, your Persian cat, your neighbor, or the garbage truck, are doing in the future:

Oh my! I will die. Tomorrow.

"Will" also expresses a strong intention -- using our will or determination -- but the difference between this and expressing the future tense is shady and hazy at times, and quite bluntly, doesn't really matter because you're using the same word:

I will (have a very strong determination to) return.

I will (simple statement of the future) return.

I mention this only because of the word "shall," which in contemporary American English, isn't such a big deal anymore, but in some rule books, lingers around. Don't worry about it. You probably don't use it because it doesn't sound natural; you've lived this long without needing it, but if you insist, this is the pedantic policy:

Use shall with I or we to express future activity; use will with I or we to express determination:

I shall eat cookies with my milk. (see? It sounds stuffy and stiff. Even I don't talk or write this way.)

I will return, and nothing will stop me! (I am expressing my determination -- my exertion of my will -- more so than announcing something I will do in the future.)

Flip flop it around with all of the other pronouns: with he, she, they, it, and one, use "will" to express something in the future tense, and "shall" to express determination:

They will eat cookies with their milk. (simple statement of something that will happen in the future)

They shall return. (determination; an order; a command)

If this doesn't make sense, don't worry about it. Nobody else does. About the only time we hear "shall" used contemporaneously is in a sentence like "Shall we dance?" or "Shall I get you a cup of tea?" In both cases, you could just as easily say, "Would you like to dance?" and "Would you like another cup of tea?"

As for "well," remember the ditty at the beginning:

"Well" rhymes with "Swell" -- and generally, when you're feeling swell, you're doing well. "Well" describes a sense of, well, well being or completion.

You look well.

The meat is well done.

I was well intentioned, but I still messed up.

To fully confirm that "well" belongs there, and not "will," replace the "well" with "won't" -- as we did earlier in this chapter -- and see if it makes sense:

You look won't. Huh?

The meat is won't done. (Too much wine before dinner, perhaps?)

I was won't intentioned, but I still messed up. That's for sure.

If won't doesn't make sense in the sentence, then will won't either.

Then and Than

"Then" rhymes with "When," and it has to do with time:

I went to the grocery store; then (when? afterwards) *I stopped by the library.*

Back then (when? 10 years ago), *gasoline was cheaper.*

After you wash the dishes, then (when? after you wash the dishes) *you can text to your heart's content.*

"Then" is also a feature of If/Then sentences, as in,

If you have the money, then (when? once you have the money) *you can buy the shoes.*

If you don't believe me, then (when? right now, if you don't believe me) *look it up for yourself.*

If you can reasonably ask, and answer, the "when?" question, then (look! it's an if/then sentence) you're probably looking at the word "Then."

"Than" is generally used when we're comparing something:

I have more books than you do.

Try to slip the "when?" question in for Than and see if it makes sense:

I have more books than (when? time doesn't come into this) *you do.*

Your latte is much stronger than mine. We are comparing two coffees, yours and mine, not talking about when anything will happen.

Are you sure that eggplant is more flavorful than zucchini?

Generally, "than" as a comparison word will be accompanied by specific comparison words like "more" or "less," or by words that imply this: taller, bigger, stronger, smellier, angrier, leaner.

And of course, because nothing in life is simple, there are sentences like this one:

Other than my bicycle, I don't have any form of transportation.

Frustratingly, this does not neatly compare something as more or less, but it most certainly does not answer the word "when" --

Other (when? this sentence has nothing to do with time) *than my bicycle, I don't have any form of transportation.*

Remembering that "then," which rhymes with "when," is used as a time marker, we choose "than" for the above sentence by process of elimination: Since we can't reasonably ask, or answer, the question "when?' in the bicycle sentence, then we use "than."

And why did we use "then" after the word "sentence" in the sentence above, by the way? You'll notice that we started with the word "Since," which is sort of like "if," which gives us a variation of the "if/then" sentence.

Why can't it be simpler? you ask. Well, from what I've heard, the entire computer world is based upon two digits, 0 and 1, which theoretically implies that anything to do with the computer is all very simple indeed.

Hah.

As you know, the English language consists of a lot more than two words.

So enough of that. Yes, it's complicated; yes, it's frustrating; yes, you'll make mistakes; no, the world won't implode because of those mistakes; and yes, it will get easier the more you do it.

Before we leave "then" and "than," let's talk about a problem some people have with "then," especially when they're explaining something chronologically:

When you make cookies, first you cream the butter and the sugar. Then you add the eggs. Then after that you put in the vanilla. Then you stir in the sifted flour, and once that's mixed in, then you add chocolate chips and then walnuts.

Bit of an overload there, wouldn't you say?

When you make cookies, first you cream the butter and the sugar, then add the eggs and vanilla. After that, you stir in the sifted flour, chocolate chips, and walnuts, one after the other.

Be aware, when you're writing, of using, and re-using the same word -- like then -- and see if there is a way that you can break things up, slip in alternative terms, or even list out the steps or bullet point them.

The purpose of writing is to convey information or a message, and you don't want irritating little things -- like the overuse of a word -- to get in the way and block people mentally from grasping that message.

Two, To, Too

More homonyms.

I put the easiest one first – the number two – and if you have trouble remembering that the numeral 2 has a "w" in the middle, try this:

Twoo Whoo! Twoo Whoo!

Owls hoot in twos!

You'll notice the "w" twice in the authenticated spelling of an owl's hoot: Twoo Whoo. This way you know that the number "two" is spelled with a "w," and you use this form of the word anyplace where you want to use the numeral 2.

Unless you're texting, you never write, "I want 2 go 2 the store," or "I want one 2!" and if you do get into this habit from texting, be aware. Be very, very aware. Bad habits don't take long to become default behavior.

Now, let's look at "to" with one "o."

Use this in two main ways (no pun intended):

First, use "to" with an action word/verb to create what we call an *infinitive* (please don't panic about the term – all it means is that you put "to" in front of a verb):

To sleep

To ponder

To die

To wonder

In Spanish, infinitives generally end in *–ar* (*hablar*), *-er* (*comer*), and *–ir* (*vivir*) and they are the base form of the verb before you attach it to I, you, he/she/it, we, or they: "I sleep," "he ponders," "they die," "we wonder."

We don't notice this much in English because our verbs look pretty much the same after everything but he/she/it, when we add "s" to the end. Officially, the process of adding specific endings to verbs depending who is doing them – I, you, he/she/it, we, they -- is called "conjugating."

You use the infinitive all the time without thinking about it, and unless you've studied Spanish, French, Italian, or Portuguese, you've probably made it fine through life without knowing what an infinitive is. But for the purpose of understanding "to," we'll talk about infinitives, just for bit:

*I need **to see** the book before I buy it.*

*The dog wants **to go** for a walk, right now.*

*Please don't forget **to pay** the newspaper deliverer before you leave for work.*

As an aside, notice that in each of the sentences above, the infinitive follows a conjugated verb – "need/to see," "wants/to go," "do not forget/to pay." Rarely do we soliloquize, "To be . . . or not to be," but occasionally, because this is English and there are no rules that apply to everything, it does happen.

Now, for the second major use of "to" with one "o" – let's think birthday presents:

To: Alexander Ignatius Philippe

From: Gwendolyn Rosemary Grace Marie

Please note that both words, "to," and "from," have one "o." As long as you remember that a gift goes "to" someone and is "from" someone else, then this random observation may jog your memory.

In our birthday gift example, "to" is used as what we call a *preposition*, which is essentially a place word, because it identifies where an item's place is – *under* the table, *over* the rainbow, *by* the chair, *in* the pot, *at* the movies. "To" is one of these place words, although (of course) when you use it, it looks slightly different –

I'm going to the store.

Next week we'll travel to Tahiti.

Give the book to the woman.

They spoke to the administrator about the excessive fees.

Loosely, you could append the question words "where?" or "who to?" before the "to" in the above sentences and make sense:

I'm going (where?) *to the store.*

Next week we'll travel (where?) *to Tahiti.*

Give the book (where?) *to the woman.*

They spoke (who to?) *to the administrator* . . .

Any time you use "to" as a preposition/place word, remember birthday presents – to: Bob, from: Jane – and remember that both "to" and "from" have one "o."

Now all that's left is too, which also has two major functions:

1) To mean "also" – I *want to go, too! Should she drop by the store too?*

You might have noticed that in the first sentence, I used a comma before "too," and in the second, I did not, and since the structure of each is pretty much the same, you're probably wondering when you're supposed to use the comma, and when not.

You may or may not be delighted – and probably will not be surprised – to learn that there is no hard and fast rule about using a comma before "too" when it's used as "also." Some people – certain high school English teachers, say – are insistent about the comma beforehand, while others – contemporary newspaper style books come to mind – are all for eliminating every comma that isn't 100 percent necessary.

Bottom line – it's your choice, influenced by whether or not you are following a particular series of style guidelines.

Now, for the second use of too:

2) **To imply excess:** *This car costs too much. It's too bad that he arrived late. There are too many cats on the porch.*

Maybe this absurd sentence will help:

*I know it seems **too** difficult **to** learn the difference between these **two** – oh, I mean three – terms.*

Oh, and how about this one:

I want a tattoo too!

(Notice how the "too" of "tattoo" is spelled the same as the "too" of "too" [also] – so as long as you remember how to spell "tattoo," this sentence will be remarkably helpful.)

Why don't we practice a bit?

1) I want two/to/too learn two/to/too drive.

2) He'll be meeting us at two/to/too o'clock.

3) Are you meeting us at the restaurant two/to/too?

4) I, two/to/too, am irritated with her.

5) It's a long way two/to/too Tipperary, wherever Tipperary is.

6) Two/To/Too doughnuts are enough for me.

7) Please give this book two/to/too the librarian.

8) This is two/to/too good two/to/too be true.

Answers:

1) I want to learn to drive. (Two infinitives, "to learn," and "to drive.")

2) He'll be meeting us at two o'clock. (The number 2.)

3) Are you meeting us at the restaurant too? (Also.)

4) I, too (also), am irritated with her.

5) It's a long way to Tipperary. ("To" used as a preposition, describing "where?")

6) Two (2) doughnuts are enough for me.

7) Please give this book to (where?) the librarian.

8) This is too (use of excess) good to be (infinitive) true.

"To" and "too," especially can be difficult to grasp, and the best way to remember them is to use whatever process of elimination works for you:

If it doesn't form an infinitive (*to eat, to wonder, to stare at*) or function as a preposition/place word (*to the store, to Bob from Margie, to Siberia*), then it's "too."

Or

If it doesn't mean also (*I want it too! He's coming, too*) or show excess (*That's too bad. They're too tired tonight*) then it's "to."

Are and Our

As with "Then" and "Than," the first step in differentiating the distinction between these two words is recognizing that they are pronounced differently:

"Are" sounds like the letter "R." If you drag out the sound long enough you sound like a pirate.

"Our" sounds like "hour." And most importantly, it looks the same, except for the "h" of "hour."

With that last sentence in mind, think on this:

Our hour of power draws near. Are you coming?

"Our" is the *possessive pronoun* of the word "we." In this possessive form, we say, "our house," "his dog," "her cookie," "their car," "your problem." Use "our" when you want to express that something belongs to us. In the case of our mnemonic sentence, we refer to "Our hour of power."

Whose hour of power?

Our hour of power.

"Are" is a verb form of "to be." Other forms of "to be" are "is," "am," "were," "was," and "been."

He is coming.

I am enraged.

They were in the front room and he was in the kitchen.

You are here; they are there; we are out of town.

In the case of "our hour of power" sentence, "are you coming?" is used as this form of "to be."

You never use "are" to say something belongs to you, as in, "Are hour of power," and if you remember to pronounce "are" like a pirate and not rhyme it with "hour," you'll remember to put "our" there.

"Our" is never used as a verb, as in, "Our you coming?" Never. Never.

WRITING MECHANICS

Now that we have dispensed with those irritating words that sound the same but don't mean the same, let's look at writing itself.

We'll begin with two more chapters on misused words that didn't fit into the previous section because, although they're frequently interchanged with one another, they don't sound the same.

From there, we'll randomly move through different aspects of writing, ranging from how to capitalize a title, which is fairly straightforward, to the more abstract, like the pitfalls of words like "should," "must," and "ought."

Remember – always remember – that the purpose behind writing is to communicate a thought, whether it is the method of making French bread or whether it is expressing your deepest love to another. You want to get your point across cleanly, clearly, and without confusion. If you keep that thought at the forefront of your mind, crowding out concerns about intransitive verbs and dangling participles, you'll stay more focused on the big picture.

Who, That, and Which

I like to put the least complicated option first:

Use "who" when you're talking about people:

He is the man who married my daughter,

As opposed to,

He is the creature that married my daughter.

As you can sense, using "that" when you're talking about people is vaguely insulting.

Regardless of how much you love animals, they are not people, and thereby do not achieve "who-ness" –

That's the dog that bit the cat that scratched the hand of the man who fed them both.

Now, "that" and "which."

There's a short, relaxed answer that will cause many grammarians to undergo apoplectic fits, and there's a longer one.

Let's start with the shorter, easier one first:

The English language is changing, and the difference between "that" and "which" is shifting as well, to the point that the words are becoming transposable:

This is the book that I was telling you about.

This is the book which I was telling you about.

Technically, "that" is correct, but if you use which, most people won't care (those who do will be the same people who insist upon answering the question, "Who is it?" with "It is I").

Now, for the longer, more complicated answer:

Use "that" when what you're talking about can't be removed from the sentence (in Grammar Speak, when you are introducing an *essential*, or *restrictive clause*).

Use "which" when what you're talking about can be removed from the sentence (GS: when you're introducing a *non-restrictive clause*). Generally, the words introduced by "which" are set off by commas.

The bicycle that was in the corner was broken.

The bicycle, which was in the corner, was broken.

Oh great. They look the same.

But they're not, really. The first sentence describes a particular bicycle – the one that was in the corner as opposed to the one that was on the sidewalk – and ironically, answers the question, "which bicycle?" (the one that was in the corner).

The second sentence tells us extra information about the bicycle – not only was it broken, but it was in the corner. This extra information is set off by commas.

Do you see why I offered the easy explanation first?

Let's try a couple more:

The painting that I bought yesterday looks perfect on my wall.

The painting, which I bought yesterday, looks perfect on my wall.

The first sentence describes a particular painting – one I bought yesterday as opposed to two weeks ago. This information is so important that it helps define the painting – if I leave it out, you won't know which painting I'm talking about: the one I bought yesterday, the one I bought two weeks ago, or the one I received as a gift at Christmas. The clause, "that I bought yesterday," is essential to the description of the painting, which is why it is called an *essential* clause.

The second sentence, however, gives bonus information about the painting that you may or may not be interested in – I bought it yesterday. The main thing I want you to know is that it looks great on my wall.

The painting looks perfect on my wall.

Let's go back to the first sentence:

The painting that I bought yesterday looks great on my wall.

If you want to replace "that" with "which," the world, and the painting, won't come crashing down:

The painting which I bought yesterday looks great on my wall.

However, in the second sentence, if you switch the "which" for "that" – it doesn't work as well:

The painting, that I bought yesterday, looks great on my wall

What we can take away from this, then, is that when we separate some information off by commas, we use "which," not "that." If the information is not separated by commas, it will probably officially require "that," but if we slip in "which" and it sounds okay to our reasonably educated ears, then we're okay.

Who and Whom

The bad news about these two words is that many people misuse them.

The good news is that, increasingly, more and more people – other than diehard grammarians – don't care.

If you're going to make a mistake, it is less of one to use "who" or "whoever" in place of "whom," or "whomever," than the other way around.

Like this:

She doesn't know who he was asking.

Whomever called had the oddest voice.

Both of the above sentences are incorrect, and should be written as such:

She doesn't know whom he was asking.

Whoever called had the oddest voice.

While the first incorrect sentence limps passably by, the second sentence sounds stilted and stiff, as if the footman were trying to speak like the butler but was doing so with a Cockney accent. It's better off to just admit that you're the footman and you're stepping in for the butler – by using "who" or "whoever" incorrectly – than it is to randomly toss "whom" or "whomever" in with your eyes closed and hope that you'll sound like you know what you're doing.

So when do you use the things?

Use "who" or "whoever" wherever you can juggle the sentence around and replace the word with I, he, she, they, or we – in Grammar Speak, the subject form of a pronoun.

Use "whom" or "whomever" where you would use me, him, her, them, or us, the object form of the pronoun.

(I don't offer "you" or "it" because these words are the same whether you use them as a subject or an object.)

Like this:

Who is on the phone? (He is on the phone.)

To whom does this belong? (This does belong to him.)

"This is the author about whom I raved." (This is the author; I raved about her.)

This is who wrote the bad check. (He wrote the bad check.)

The juggling thing is awkward, I know. Try to keep as many of the words as you can, regardless of their order, and slip in the he/him, she/her, I/me options and see which one sounds best.

Generally, if there is a verb – an action word like eat, sleep, read, think, or a deceptively action word like is, are, has, does – hanging around without a corresponding subject word that is doing whatever the action is, then "who" or "whoever" will fit in:

I saw who ate the last piece of cake.

In the sentence above, "I" is the subject word doing the action "saw" – I saw – but other than "who," there's no other subject option for "ate."

Didn't she tell you who called last night?

"She" goes with "didn't tell." "Who" goes with "called."

Now let's make a minor change and see what a difference it makes:

Didn't she tell you whom she called last night?

Well, now the verb "called" has a noun, "she," to go with it, and "whom" is kicking around on its own. If you do the switching words around thing, you'll get,

. . . she called him/her/us as opposed to . . . she called he/she/we, so you'll slip "whom" into the sentence as opposed to "who."

If this gives you a headache, I sympathize. And if you wrote the sentence like this,

Didn't she tell you who she called last night?

many people, including your software grammar check, won't notice or care.

There is a reason why the difference between "who" and "whom" is becoming negligible, in the same way that we no longer distinguish between the informal "thee" and "thou" and the informal "ye" and "you."

If language never changed, Shakespeare's English would be considered wildly modern.

Let's practice:

1) She will give the package to whoever/whomever arrives first.

2) Our boss, who/whom is late as usual, told us all to be early.

3) The four girls, one of who/whom was my sister, went to the movies.

4) Who/Whom goes there?

5) Who/Whom is it?

6) Is it she who/whom you invited?

7) Is it she who/whom invited you?

Answers:

1) She will give the package to whoever arrives first. ("Arrives" is an action word/verb that needs a subject, like "She arrives first," so "whoever" fits)

2) Our boss, who is late as usual, told us all to be early. (Another action word/verb – is – needing a subject word – "He is late as usual")

3) The four girls, one of whom was my sister, went to the movies. ("One" is the subject word accompanying "was" – you would also say, "one of them" as opposed to "one of they")

4) Who goes there? (He goes there. "Who" functions as the subject word for the action word/verb "goes")

5) Who is it? (Same as above. Words like "is," "are," "was," "were," "has," and "had" are verbs that many people miss because they don't see the "action" part about them)

6) Is it she whom you invited? (You invited her. Use "whom" when you can juggle the words around and fit in her/him/them/me/us)

7) Is it she who invited you? (She invited you. Use "who" when you can juggle the words around and fit in she/he/they/I/we)

I wish that there were a ditty or an easy answer that I could give you, but short of taking time to learn the difference between the nominative case (the subject, like I/she/he/we/they – this is when you use "who" or "whoever") and the accusative (the object, like me/her/him/us/them – this is when you use "whom" or "whomever"), there is no easy answer.

Formal versus Informal Writing

Generally, writing is thought to be more formal than speech.

While we may say, "What's up?" or "How's it going?" if we were writing the same question, even in an e-mail, we would be more likely to phrase it, "How are you?"

However, even when we speak, we adjust the level of formality depending upon to whom we are speaking (formal speech) or who we are speaking to (informal speech):

"So, where're we goin' to?" which we might ask a family member or best friend, turns into,

"Where are we going?" when we're talking to our boss.

In the same way, writing varies in its level of formality, depending upon what you are writing and to whom it is addressed. Where once a note card to a friend or a memo predominated as examples of informal writing, nothing today beats out texting, which has to be the ultimate (so far) in relaxed communication:

C u soon.

On the opposite spectrum is the PhD dissertation, which not only abounds in pedantic, prescriptive style, but requires specific, unyielding adherence to guidelines on punctuation, footnotes, bibliographic references, and even line spacing and depth of the first-line indent. (To make it worse, there is no agreed upon guideline for these dissertations, this being based upon the whim of the individual university body conferring the degree.)

And then there's everything in between.

Which means – and this shouldn't surprise us – that there is no one rule for formal writing and one rule for informal, because there is no universal statute as to which is which, and what makes one formal and one informal, and when we use either.

But we can use our common sense.

If you are writing a business letter, it will probably be formal; if you are writing a personal letter, it will be less so.

If you are writing an e-mail to the CEO of your company, it will be formal; if you are writing to a friend, it will be less so.

If you are writing a paper for your English 101 class, it will be formal; if you are writing a story for a child, it will or will not be less so (Beatrix Potter's children's books come to mind; anyone who uses words like "soporific" or sentences like, "He implored him to exert himself," is not emphasizing casual).

The circumstances dictate the action.

Here are some things to keep in mind about formal writing:

1) **Stay in the third person** – he, she, it – as opposed to using "you" – "The potato is not necessarily the horrible vegetable it is accused of being," as opposed to, "The potato isn't as bad as you think it is."

2) **Write out words as opposed to using contractions** -- "It will be done by tomorrow," instead of, "It'll be done tomorrow."

3) **Forgo abbreviations** – Use "photograph" instead of "photo," or "pic," "television" instead of TV, although "digital versatile disc" (DVD) would have many people stumped. If, as in this latter case, the abbreviation is so common that nobody recognizes what it stands for, then use the abbreviation.

4) **Watch slang or informalisms** –"kick butt," "smart ass," "wicked!"

5) **Avoid colloquial words** – Use "going to" instead of "gonna," "children" instead of "kids," "man" instead of "guy." You don't have to get weird about this – as in employing "wordsmith" instead of "writer," or "pedagogue" instead of "teacher." Use your common sense.

6) **Don't order your reader around with what we call the Imperative Voice** – "Eat your broccoli," "Pay the telephone bill," or "Quit kicking the dog." Rather, "It is important for people to eat their

broccoli," "The telephone bill must be paid," and, "It is unnecessary to kick the dog."

7) **Use complete sentences as opposed to fragments** – "Not in my house" becomes, "This does not happen in my house."

The longer your sentences (provided that they are correctly punctuated), the more formal they sound, but you can still be formal and concise at the same time.

What we're effectively talking about here is tone, and anybody who has raised a teenager (or been one) knows that something as simple as the word "yes" can be infused with all sorts of emotion and meaning, depending upon body language, eye rolling, and voice level.

Similarly, your writing adopts a tone – ranging from languidly casual to starchedly stiff necked, depending upon word choice and placement, sentence construction, and intimacy.

Use your best judgment. Read your work aloud – if you would not speak to the reader with the level of informality that you're hearing, then you most certainly would not write to them in that manner.

If you are going to err (and you will, because you're human), it is better to do so on the side of being more formal than less. It's better to be called haughty than insolent, especially when the person making that observation has the power to hire or fire you.

By the way, in case you were wondering, this book is written in an informal, yet reserved tone. You, my readers, are not my buddies or pals, and I do my best to not address you as if we were. Neither, however, are you on the hiring committee, so I do not have to keep you at arm's length.

You notice that I use "you," which is found in more informal writing. I do not, however, employ "wanna," "gotta," or even "got to," which is how I would express myself around the dinner table with my children.

One of my favorite writers for tone (and content, actually) is C.S. Lewis, whose landmark book, *Mere Christianity*, puts in written form a series of radio talks that the author gave during the German blitz bombing of London during World War II. Lewis was asked to provide a sequence of warm, friendly, encouraging talks to a people who were, mildly putting it, scared.

Later, Lewis transposed these talks into written form, keeping the same warm, friendly tone. While this won't work for a PhD dissertation, it does translate well into blogs, certain informational articles, and letters. At the very least, it's delightful to read. Try it.

Varying Your Sentence Structure

Without recognizing it, you can easily fall into a repetitive pattern of formulating your sentences:

The dog is an interesting creature. It is man's best friend. The dog waits for its master. It is not like a cat. A cat is not as friendly as a dog. Many people prefer dogs over cats. Dogs are friendlier.

This extreme example -- of short, elementary sentences creating something that looks like a second-grader's first essay -- is to emphasize the point:

All of these sentences are structured the same way, which in grammarian-speak is subject/predicate, or more colloquially, Somebody/What Somebody Is or Did:

The dog (somebody)/*is an interesting creature* (what somebody is or did).

It (somebody)/*is man's best friend* (what somebody is or did).

The dog (somebody)/*waits for its master* (what somebody is or did).

A collection of these sentences, one after the other, written in the same manner, sounds stilted, boring, and childish, but solving the problem is relatively easy. First, consider using joining words, officially called conjunctions: and, but, or, for, nor, so, yet (by the way, if you say these seven words in the same order, over and over again, you'll eventually memorize them. When you want to memorize something, do it in the same order, every time, and make it easier on yourself):

A dog is an interesting creature and man's best friend.

The dog waits for its master, but the cat lives for itself.

Dogs are friendlier than cats, and many people prefer dogs over cats.

This is a great start to add more interest to your writing. Now, take the next step, and consider beginning a sentence with a word or words like "after," "because," "with," "even though," "despite" -- and you'll enter a new dimension:

Because a dog is friendlier than a cat, many people prefer owning a dog.

You can also achieve complexity, and interest, by combining elements from a series of simple sentences into one longer, more dense phrase:

Man's best friend, the friendly and eager dog lives to please its master. Unlike the cat, which seems cool and aloof, the dog jumps up and follows its master wherever that master goes.

Doesn't that sound better?

Of course, you can take this too far:

Because it is a hallmark of the nature of the species to be friendly and open, members of the canine family exhibit a strong pre-disposition toward a gregariousness that leads to their being preferred -- overwhelmingly -- to cats, by the humans who make these sort of decisions.

This sentence -- while it is grammatically correct and appropriately punctuated -- is too much for the subject matter. Your goal, in varying your sentence structure, is the same goal you've always had: to get your message across clearly and openly. A supercilious, artificially intellectualized writing style -- laden with multi-syllabic words and dense structure -- is just as bad as the opposite, a series of painfully short, woefully elementary phrases that chop chop chop their way into the reader's brain.

How do you know when you are erring either way, you ask? Try this:

1) **Read your work aloud.** See how it sounds. Is there a sing/song cadence that alerts you to the overused subject/predicate structure? Or are you

stumbling over words because they are too long, too many, too complicated?

2) **Give your work to someone else to read.** Do they get what you're trying to say? Are they interested enough to read through to the end? Is there anything glaring that jumps out at them? (Be aware -- it's very difficult to watch someone else read the product of your hard work -- but if your message isn't getting through, you really want to know.)

3) **Develop an innate, interior sense of good writing by reading a lot of it yourself.** Good writers are avid readers, and they are impatient with bad writing. It bothers them. Here's another thing of which to be aware: just because a book is at the top of the best seller list does not ensure that it is well written. More than once, I have attempted a book recommended by someone in their mid-teens -- many of these tomes have been made into movies, extolled for their story and their writing. I can't read them. They drive me nuts. Style, tone, subject matter, characterization -- there is a marked dumbing down in quality. If you find that you are getting impatient with a book, the problem does not necessarily lie with you.

Please don't panic about this. Remember -- always -- that you have something to say, and your goal is to write it in such a way that people grasp the message. The more you do this, the easier it will become. While it seems overwhelming at first, just move forward -- steadily, slowly, persistently -- and you will progress.

As an added bonus, you may find that the more you focus on improving your writing, the better you speak as well. The time you spend analyzing and critiquing your written words is time well spent, because as you practice slowing down and reviewing your words before you set them down on paper, you begin to do the same thing before you blurt them out of your mouth.

I was especially gratified to see this starting to happen in my own life, because I literally speak as I think, which tends to be disastrous more than it does beneficial. Hours and hours of editing and reviewing what I type spills over in my daily speech, and there is a micro-second's pause before what is born in my brain emerges into somebody else's ears.

What Is a Sentence?

Life holds many deep questions, and while I recognize that the one in the title may not be one you have pondered as you view the heavens and wonder why you are here, it is a difficult question to address, simply because, like everything else in life, the answer isn't simple. Let's try, though.

In the last chapter on Varying Your Sentence Structure, we talked about the concept of subject/predicate, or Somebody/What Somebody Is or Did.

In order for a sentence to qualify as a sentence, it needs a subject – Somebody, and a predicate – What Somebody Is or Did. Here are some examples of sentences:

Bob (somebody) *fell down the stairs* (what Bob did).

Eddie the ugly cat (somebody) *sleeps on the porch all day* (what Eddie does, which, frankly, isn't much of anything).

Cake and cookies (somebody, in this case, something) *are on the table* (what something is doing – being on the table).

Anna, her brother, her brother's uncle, her brother's uncle's dog, and the dog's puppies (somebody, a lot of them) *slept under the porch Tuesday night* (what somebodies did).

Algernon (somebody) *ran down the stairs, tripped over a bicycle in the middle of the sidewalk, flew through the air, smashed into a tree, and broke his arm* (what somebody, quite unfortunately, did).

You'll notice that, in all of these examples, Somebody comes first, and what they did, second. I'm sure it won't surprise you to learn that it isn't always that simple.

Will you stop by the post office on your way back from work?

So who's the Somebody in this sentence, which happens to be in question form? To find out, let's change it from a question to a statement:

You will stop by the post office on your way back from work.

Now you can see that the Somebody is "You" and what you did is "will stop by the post office on your way back from work." What's confusing is that, when you look at the sentence in its question form, the Somebody – you – is squeezed between "Will" and "stop." How frustrating.

But once you realize this, and you're faced with a question, you can put it back in its statement form and see if you can identify the Somebody and What Somebody Did:

Why didn't the cupcakes turn out?

The cupcakes (Somebody) *didn't turn out why?* (What Somebody Did).

Although the question sounds awkward in statement form, the key thing is that we've discovered Somebody and What Somebody Did, and we realize we have a complete sentence.

Sentences quickly get really complicated –

For many years after the flood, the trees along the bank shivered and shook every time there was a wind whistling through their leaves, and the flowers turned pale, all of the color disappearing from their blossoms.

But we don't have to panic about it. Start with the simple stuff and work your way to more difficult. In the case of the above sentence, there are a couple Somebodies – "the trees" ("along the bank" gives us a more specific definition of just which trees we're talking about) and "the flowers."

What "the trees" did was shiver and shake; "the flowers" turned pale. All of the rest of the words add detail and dimension – which is extremely frustrating when we're trying to figure out the function of the words in the sentence, but most gratifying when we're reading or speaking. Can you imagine how mind numbingly boring it would be if every sentence we spoke was along the lines of

William married Kate. It was a nice wedding. The Queen was pleased. Everybody cheered.

We already discussed this in Varying Your Sentence Structure. It's important to not sound like, or write like, eight-year-olds.

Now that we've talked a bit about what a sentence is, let's discuss non-sentences, which are generally called fragments. Because they are missing either a subject – Somebody, or predicate – What Somebody Did, fragments are incomplete sentences, potential sentences, if you will:

Bob. (Somebody. Nothing else.)

Ate the entire cake. (What Somebody -- Bob, maybe? -- Did, but we don't know who Somebody is.)

After six p.m. (We see no Somebody, nor What Somebody Did. This is called a phrase – a collection of related words that has no subject and no predicate.)

While these are more obvious examples, fragments are not always easy to spot (of course):

If you eat the entire chocolate cake.

So what's the problem? "You" is Somebody and "eat the entire cake" is What Somebody Did. That would be true if it weren't for the unfortunate addition of that little word, "If," which turns what would otherwise be a complete sentence into something we call an *insubordinate clause*. Others words to look out for in this vein are "after," "before," "while," "when," and other relatives, which set up a sentence, but don't quite complete it.

Don't worry about what it's called – just try to recognize it when you see one:

After I arrived at the airport. This clause is missing both a Somebody, and What Did Somebody Do? If we want to turn it into a proper sentence, we will need to add those elements. Like this, for example:

After I arrived at the airport, the baggage carousel (Somebody) *broke down* (What Somebody Did).

Here's another clause, without a Somebody and What Somebody Did:

When you called me last night.

Now let's fix it:

When you called me last night, I (Somebody) *was so tired* (What Somebody Did) *that I couldn't think straight enough to answer your questions.*

Another one:

Three hours before the movie started. (What happened? What did Somebody Do?)

Three hours before the movie started, two cats (Somebody*) entered the theater* (What Somebody Did) *and ate all the popcorn in the concession stand* (more of What Somebody Did).

The hard part about these clauses is that they look like they are talking about a Somebody and a Somebody Doing Something, as in *Three hours before the movie started*:

"The movie" is Somebody and "started" is What Somebody Did, you say.

Well, true, but there's the "Three hours before" part that messes everything up and turns what would be a complete sentence into a clause.

If you use your common sense, you can see that these fragments don't express complete thoughts, and we are left dangling, frustrated from a lack of information.

I said at the beginning of the chapter that sentences were complicated things, and they are, and most of our problems with sentence structure and that dreaded concept of . . .

punctuation

arise from writing incomplete sentences, and putting them together the wrong way.

But before you panic, think about this: you can speak, and probably quite well. Unless you are one of those rare terse persons who conserve words as if they were air bubbles under water --

Ate great meal.

Tired. Must sleep.

Good book. Recommend it.

you tend to naturally speak in complete sentences without thinking about it. And if you can speak in complete sentences, then you can write them as well.

The examples above look like Tweets or text messages, and now that we've introduced the subject, this is as good a time as any to discuss what Twitter, and other social media, are doing to our language skills.

Check out Twitter – but not too long; you've honestly got better things to do – and notice how many fragments and non-sentences there are. Given the limited number of characters you are allowed, it only makes sense that you'll rapidly start dropping things: first, articles (the, a, an), then pronouns (I, he, we), prepositions (of, after, behind), and then a rapidly escalating series of words that add depth to our writing and impact to our speaking, so that what starts out like this:

By the time you read this, I will have been in Hawaii for six hours, lazing in the sun, sipping tea, and generally wishing you were here but being glad that I'm not there.

Turns into this:

In Hawaii sipping tea wish u were here

While it's understandable given the limitation of Tweets, it's also dangerous, in that it trains us to be brusque, clipped, and abbreviated, and if we write this way too much, it starts to sound normal. Just keep an eye on it, okay?

Now, before we leave this chapter, I want to introduce a few examples that sort of look like sentences, but really aren't:

He bought.

We reviewed.

Amanda values.

Using our criteria of subject/Somebody and predicate/What Somebody Does, it initially looks like these should be sentences, although something inside our brain tells us that they don't sound right. We should listen to our brain.

Yes, "he" is Somebody and "bought" is what Somebody Did, but it doesn't tell the whole story: what did he buy?

"We" are Somebody and "reviewed" is What We Did, but what did we review? And as for Amanda, what does she value?

In Grammar Speak, "bought," "reviewed," and "values" are considered *transitive verbs*. Transitive verbs are those that are not complete unless they have what is called a *direct object*, which basically answers the What? question that keeps coming up:

He bought a pet snake. ("Snake" is the direct object, answering the question, "What did he buy?")

We reviewed the documents. ("Documents" is the direct object, answering the question, "What did we review?

Amanda values honest, hardworking people. (What does Amanda value? People – direct object. As an aside, and if you're ready for this, "honest" and "hardworking" tell us more about – or modify – the word "people." In the World of Grammar these are called *adjectives*.)

Verbs that do not require an answer to What? are called intransitive verbs:

Timothy Elliot travels.

They laughed.

I slept.

Despite these being very short sentences, they are indeed sentences, because the question What? does not come into factor. "Timothy Elliot" – Somebody, "travels," – What Somebody Does. The information is complete, as is the sentence, and nothing needs to be added.

They -- Somebody, *laughed* – What Somebody Did.

I – Somebody, *slept* – What Somebody Did.

And because nothing in life, or the English language, is simple, some words can be both transitive – requiring a direct object, or an answer to the question What? – and intransitive – able to stand alone and not requiring a direct object:

We ate.

We ate cookies.

They read.

They read books.

Guinevere drives.

Guinevere drives a blue car.

"Ate," "read," and "drives" are examples of verbs that arc both transitive and intransitive.

While this may seem overwhelming, it's really not, because – in the same way that you naturally speak in complete sentences, you also regularly answer the What? question when you are faced with a transitive verb. If you're not sure, strip the whole sentence down to its undies – its basic subject/Somebody and predicate/What Somebody Does or Did, and see if it still makes sense:

Every third Thursday, the sweet little old lady who lives down the street from my parents purchases.

Who's Somebody? Well, it's not Thursday, third or otherwise, and while she may be sweet, little, and old, ultimately we're talking about "lady." The "who" that follows this word alerts us that we're introducing a dependent clause – "who lives down the street from my parents" – that doesn't stand up on its own,

So what does the lady *do*?

Purchases.

What does she purchase?

That What? question tells us that we've got a transitive verb, hanging around on the corner by itself, ready to cause trouble because it doesn't have a direct object to give it a sense of purpose and completion. All we have to do to fix the problem is tell the reader what the sweet little old lady purchases:

Every third Thursday, the sweet little old lady who lives down the street from my parents purchases new sheets for her bed.

What an expensive habit.

Despite this being the longest chapter in the book, we've only breathed lightly on the subject of what is, or is not, a sentence, simply because there are so many variables. Even when you know all the grammar, and the appropriate terms, there are arguments as to whether such and so is a valid sentence, and why or why not.

Again, listen to your ear – it's highly likely that you naturally speak in complete sentences.

And follow this up by reading as much quality literary work as you can – keeping in mind that not all newspapers or published books necessarily adhere strongly to correct writing and punctuation technique – and you will start to absorb, through mental osmosis, what feels and looks "right."

Paragraphs Matter

Have you ever seen a facsimile of the Declaration of Independence?

The handwriting itself, while gorgeous, is difficult for the 21st century eye to decipher, but what makes it worse is that there are loooooooooonnnnnnnnggggg lines, stacked one upon the other, with nary a break. It's easy to get lost, mid-line, and not find your way back again.

Now, pick up a newspaper and glance through the front page. It's pretty likely that no more than three sentences go by before someone hit the paragraph indent key, and sometimes, there's only one sentence.

There are two principle reasons why we use paragraphs:

1) **To cluster like ideas together in a unit.**

2) **To break up blocks of text so that they are easy to read.**

Depending upon what you are writing, you will probably need no more than five sentences in a paragraph, and depending upon how you are publishing your work, you may use less.

Newspapers break sentences into paragraphs on a fairly frequent basis because their columns are narrow, and five sentences worth of copy may result in a 6-8 inch column of unbroken type. The eye craves white space in the midst of black type, and if it can't find it, it skips elsewhere -- to a photo, say.

In a book with columns 3-5 inches wide, those same five sentences don't look nearly as imposing. What with the indentations at the beginning of each paragraph and the varied extra white space at the end of each sentence, there's enough visual breakup to keep the reader from feeling overwhelmed. (By the way, it's not mandatory to indent the first line of a paragraph; you'll notice that I don't. You can also identify a paragraph by skipping a line.)

So if you're writing a letter to a client talking about a new product that you have just developed, your nice wide piece of paper means that you have pleasantly wide columns, and only need to break for paragraphs when you introduce a new topic:

Dear Client:

Last month at Steve Henderson Fine Art, we launched our line of signed, limited edition prints, and every month we add to the collection. Prints are limited to runs of 200; they are hand-signed and numbered individually by the artist; and are accompanied by a certificate of authenticity.

Printed on archival quality paper with archival quality inks, the prints are affordably priced and are available in a selection of sizes. We offer them unframed -- so that you may take them to your favorite professional framer -- or matted and framed from our studio. Shipping with either option is free.

Whether you are looking for a landscape, a coastal scene, still life, or a figurative work, we have the right print, in the right size, for the right price, for your walls.

Sincerely,

In the letter above, I broke from the first paragraph -- introducing the prints and describing their limited run -- to the second, which focuses on the physical attributes of the prints themselves. If my letter had been introducing both limited edition prints and open edition posters, I may have chosen to fuse paragraphs 1 and 2 together, and broken for the separate topic of the open edition posters, after the sentence, "Shipping is free" --

We are also excited to introduce a growing selection of Steve's works as posters, which you may purchase with or without inspirational sayings.

Sometimes, it's easy to determine that you're talking about a new topic, but other times, it's not. As with many aspects of writing the English language, when to break for a paragraph is sometimes an arbitrary decision, and what you think is right may not be --

and frequently isn't -- in accordance with your extremely inflexible, pedantic English instructor.

Just remember -- always remember -- that the primary purpose behind things like punctuation and breaking for paragraphs and correct spelling is CLARITY. You want your message to get through. You want your message to be clearly and easily accessible to your reader. You also want it to be laid out in such a fashion that your reader's eye is not strained as he reads your words -- a graphic design element, incidentally, that was totally unimportant to grammarians of the 19th century who propounded some of the rules that we, 150 years later, still struggle with.

Do people understand what you're saying? Do the paragraph breaks make sense -- topic-wise -- without being too frequent (every single solitary sentence is its own paragraph) or too few (big black block of print)? As long as you are out of high school and college essay classes, you are less interested in getting an "A" for fulfilling an individual instructor's arbitrary requirements as you are conveying to your reader -- clearly and easily -- your message.

Before we leave this chapter, let's talk about conversation and paragraphs, and you'll be happy to know that there's a hard and fast rule that you can follow on this one:

When people talk, change paragraphs every time you change speakers:

"I don't understand this paragraph thing," she moaned.

"I know," he replied. "It can be frustrating."

"So you get frustrated, too?"

"Sometimes, but I keep at it, as I do with anything. Nothing worth doing well comes easily, but the more you practice, the better you get."

"That's a relief."

You can look back at the five lines and start with "she," then "he," "she," "he," "she," and because each person receives a different line, you don't have to keep saying, "she said," "he replied," and "she agonized."

Of course, if someone is making a long speech, then your arbitrary rules of breaking into paragraphs based upon subject matter, applies:

"I don't understand this paragraph thing," she moaned.

"I know," he replied. "It can be frustrating.

"I have found, however, that the more I practice something, the better I get at it. And once I do attain a

level of mastery, I find myself wanting to learn more and more."

The second and third lines are spoken by the same person, "he," and you'll notice that after the word "frustrating" at the end of the second line, there is no quotation mark. At the beginning of the third line, "I have found," however, there is a quotation mark.

Quick rule here:

Start and end quotes with quotation marks:

"I am so frustrated," she said. "This is really difficult."

If the same person starts another paragraph and is still speaking, leave off the quotation mark at the end of the paragraph break:

"I am so frustrated.

"This is really difficult."

The reader understands that the same person is speaking, without the necessity of irritating repetition:

"I am so frustrated," she said.

"This is really difficult," she said.

Does this seem overwhelming? Please don't let it be so -- always remember that the ultimate purpose behind the various rules is clarity of communication, and when clarity isn't an issue anymore, things change. That's why we no longer use the words "thee" and "thou" to differentiate the informal "you" from the formal "ye" and "you" -- at some point, it didn't matter to most people anymore, and we eventually -- as a people -- dropped it.

Capitalize the Word "I"

This is a short chapter, and if you're over the age of 40, you probably don't need it, but in these days of texting, we've got a problem with the word "I."

You know what i think?

Later in the day i will be by with the papers.

He and i will look into this later.

When you're texting, it's a pain to figure out how to capitalize a word in the middle of the sentence, so people don't. I understand that. It takes me 10 minutes to compose a text to my daughters which they answer back in 30 seconds: "What were u doing? ive been waiting for your answer."

Texting is one thing. Everything else is another.

Always, always, always capitalize "I" when you are talking about yourself:

I am a slow texter.

If you send me the papers, I will read them.

Tomorrow I will pick up some ice-cream.

Always.

How Do You Capitalize a Title?

Songs, books, movies, chapter headings -- we use titles all the time, and there are specific rules for capitalizing them.

First, and easiest -- always capitalize the first word:

How do you capitalize a title?

And the last word:

How do you capitalize a Title?

Third, capitalize everything that isn't

1) **an article** (the, a, an)

2) **a preposition** (of, with, by, near, over, under, around, beneath -- basically a place word that defines where something is)

3) **the word, "to"** -- which can be used as a preposition (see number 2) or the beginning of what is called the infinitive form of a verb (to eat, to see, to play, to run, to capitalize) -- for all practical purposes just remember not to capitalize the word "to"

4) **a conjunction** (and, but, or, for, nor, so, yet -- we chatted about these in the chapter on Varying Your Sentence Structure)

How Do You Capitalize a Title?

or, to choose something more complicated:

The Man, the Woman, an Errant Boy in the Sand, and a Little Girl Who Wanted to Stand behind the Wardrobe Door but Didn't Know How To

The first word, The, is capitalized. All of the other "the's" are not. Neither are the two other articles, "a," and "an."

Also uncapitalized are "and" and "but" because they are conjunctions (and, but, or, for, nor, so yet).

The same goes for the preposition placement words, "in," "to," and "behind," but not the last "to," because it is the last word of the title.

Long prepositions, like "behind," "above," "below," "underneath," may be capitalized for no other reason than that they have so many letters in them -- it's optional, with the general rule being that if they consist of four or fewer letters, you keep them lowercase, but if they have five or more letters, you may capitalize them, or not. There's some sense of relief in knowing that you've got some choice in the matter.

Within the body of a work, you identify a title by either placing it within quotes: "The Title Is in between Quotes," or *italicizing* it. Again, your preference, unless the place you are writing for has specific style recommendations (many newspapers, for some odd reason, do not italicize titles, a throwback, perhaps, to the days when it was difficult to typeset in italics. How long has that been? Thirty years?)

General Rules for Capitalizing

I'm sure it won't come as a surprise that there are a number of rules regarding which words to capitalize, and like all rules, there are exceptions. Rather than trying to cover all of our bases, let's just look at some of the major ones. If you keep up on these, you should be fine with 92 percent of the general populace.

Capitalize the following:

1) **The first word of a sentence.** Always. Even if it's a fragment, which technically isn't a sentence. But if it starts after a period, then capitalize it. You'll notice that "the," "always," "even," and "but" were capitalized in this paragraph, even though the only true sentence is the last one, the one beginning with "but." If you do not capitalize anything else in any of your writing, please do remember this one. I have waded through blogs that look like this:

teapots and teacups break when you drop them. so the best thing is not to drop them. of course, if you drop them on a soft carpet, they probably won't break. why, however, take the chance?

This drives me nuts. I want to scream, "Just capitalize the first letter of each sentence or fragment. Please!"

Why does this matter? Go back to the italicized writing above and read it -- do you find it mildly difficult to see when one sentence starts and ends? That little period is mighty small and easy to miss;

capitalizing the first word of each sentence or fragment makes it easier to determine when each one of those sentences or fragments begins.

2) **In the previous "Just capitalize" sentence, you'll notice that I capitalized the J of "just," which was the first word in a quotation.** Treat a quotation, even if it's in the body of the sentence, as a separate sentence of its own, and capitalize the first word in it. Then, within the quotation, remember to capitalize the beginning of each sentence.

3) **People's names -- first, last, middle.** If it's their name, capitalize it.

4) **Names of continents, countries, streets, towns, states:** North America, France, Sixth Avenue, Walla Walla, Idaho. These are specific names, as if the places were people. Words like meadow, countryside, river, mountain, unless attached to a specific name (The Blue Ribbon River) are not capitalized, the same way that you don't capitalize boy, woman, man, police officer, writer, artist.

5) **Days of the week and months of the year.** Holidays -- Christmas, New Year, Halloween.

6) **Mr., Mrs., Ms., Dr., Father (as in a priest)** -- if it's a title before their name, capitalize it, because technically it's part of their name. President Bob McFaddian, but Bob McFaddian, president. The first one is capitalized because it forms part of Bob's name; the second is not, because it describes who Bob is. Confusing? I know.

There are more, but if you can remember these -- especially number one, and number three would be nice as well, you should get by.

e e cummings -- the poet famous, or infamous, for eschewing capitalization and punctuation -- aside, capitalizing is simply a tool to help us break down all that print matter and keep it from running all together. When something is capitalized, we're basically saying, "Stop! This is important because this is the beginning of a sentence. Or it's a person's name, like Carolyn Henderson, and she matters because she is unique and one of a kind. Or because she's Polish, which describes her as a descendent from a specific place, in this case Poland, which isn't just any country but a very unique one, separate from, say, France or Thailand or Iceland."

Sometimes you may slip in a word that doesn't need to be capitalized, again, like president, as in, "The President of the knitting group got up to speak." You don't need to capitalize this, because "president" isn't part of the person's name, as in, "President Bartholomew Williams handed the gavel to his vice president, Guinevere Jameson," but if you accidentally do so, the walls probably won't come crashing down.

The same goes for a word like "river," as in, "The River was running high this morning." There's no reason to capitalize "river" in this case because it's not naming a specific river, as in, "The Columbia River that separates Washington and Oregon," but if you do so, dreadful things will probably not happen.

Is It a Sin to End a Sentence with a Preposition?

No.

Look up, "ending a sentence with a preposition" on the Internet sometime and you will overwhelmingly come to the conclusion that this rule isn't really a rule at all. While it is true that, in Latin, ending a sentence with a preposition is a huge no-no, we don't speak Latin.

However, because so many of us have been told, from the cradle, "Never end a sentence with a preposition," (by the way, always be skeptical of sentences that being with "never"), we recoil when we see sentences like this in written form:

Who were you talking to?

She told me what the movie is about.

The doctor is in.

He left because he was tired of being put down.

I'm not sure what they are looking at.

We don't think twice when people speak these sentences, and only the most grammatically repressed mentally change them to,

To whom were you talking?

About the movie's plot, she told me.

In the doctor is.

Of being put down, he was tired.

At what they are looking, I am not sure.

Even when we're dealing with the difference between informal speech and more formal writing, these re-writes sound stilted and unnatural, with the possible exception of the first one.

One of the observations our Spanish-speaking friends make about English is that we tack prepositions onto simple words to create totally new meanings. Consider all of the prepositions that you can add to the end of the word "look," all of which, effectively, create new words:

Look up (as a word, in the dictionary)

Look into (the matter)

Look at

Look over

Look around

Look out

All of these informal, composite words can be replaced by more formal synonyms – Look up/find a word; look into/research the matter; look at/observe the sunset; look over/review the facts; look around/reconnoiter the landscape; look out (for)/beware (of) bears. Sometimes the more formal synonym sounds better, but just as often it doesn't, not quite capturing the nuances of the colloquialism.

"I'll take a look around," has a totally different feeling than, "I will perform reconnaissance activities."

One of the major arguments against ending a sentence with a preposition – other than that we're all told never to do so – is that it weakens the sentence, substituting a more powerful, descriptive verb with an all purpose word tacked anemically onto a preposition.

Well, sometimes this is true, and sometimes it isn't.

What other stories will you think up?

Whether you put "think up" at the end of the sentence or in the middle ("You think up some interesting stories,"), in formal writing you'd probably want to consider a stronger, more descriptive way of expressing yourself:

What other imaginative stories will you create? This sort of says the same thing, but more circumspectly. It also sounds more formal.

I cannot, however, argue with "come up with," which has the dubious distinction of not one, but two prepositions at its end:

What other stories will you come up with?

So, "think up," is weak; "create," works; but "come up with," – double BAD Preposition NoNo! – is a surprisingly good choice.

It's your call. Just be aware of three things:

1) When you end a sentence with a preposition, people will be sure to let you know.

2) There is no official rule of grammar concerning ending a sentence with a preposition.

3) If, however, you find that you make a regular habit of ending sentences with prepositions, be aware of this – while you're not breaking a rule, you may be too heavily depending upon informal, colloquial speech, weakening your writing by not seeking out single word, descriptive alternatives.

Is It a Sin to Begin a Sentence with a Conjunction?

You know, with all the truly awful things that we are capable of doing to cause angst and damage in other people's lives, it's really too bad that we feel inordinately anxious about something like this.

No, it's not a sin to begin a sentence with a conjunction, unless, or course, you are writing for a really uptight English teacher.

Do I pick on these people?

Oh well, too bad. Too many adults have bad memories of blood-red written essay offerings, ripped to shreds and splattered with exclamatory notes like, "FRAGMENT!" or "NEVER begin a sentence with a conjunction!" with the result that they go through life saying, "I can't write. I don't know what a noun is. I don't know how to write."

The good English teachers -- the ones who care about content as much, or more, than technique and realize how easy it is to squash a budding writer's enthusiasm -- don't do this, and thankfully, good English teachers exist. But so do bad ones, and if you were unfortunate enough to have one, it's time to get his or her voice out of your head and red pen off of your desk and get back to expressing yourself again.

But I digress.

We were talking about whether or not you can begin a sentence with a conjunction -- and, but, or, for, nor, so, yet -- which is what I did in the paragraph above.

And the answer is, yes, you can.

But it's not something you want to do all the time.

Or even frequently.

Beginning a sentence with a conjunction is a, "Stop! I'm making a point, here," move, and you reserve it for times when you want the reader to, well, stop, and look at the point you're trying to make.

If you do it too much, you lose any impact you initially made by overuse, and the reader no longer stops and pays especial attention to what you are saying.

Some people say that it is acceptable to begin a sentence with a conjunction in only informal writing, and that formal prose -- as in a dissertation or business letter or academic treatise -- requires that we refrain from doing so.

But even in these types of writing, the technique of "Stop! This is important!" achieved through beginning a sentence with a conjunction applies.

Just be aware that some people may frown upon this (the head of the dissertation committee comes to mind), and think twice before you do so.

Overuse of Would, Can, and Could

Some people just have trouble being assertive. Making a simple, declarative sentence is difficult for them, to the point that they will not write,

I want the chocolate cookie.

But rather,

I would like the chocolate cookie.

Subconsciously, they are telling themselves that "would" softens the demand, but in reality, it weakens the sentence, and when a series of "woulds," "cans," and "coulds" splatters through the prose, things get really irritating, really fast:

I would prefer arriving tomorrow but I could see about looking into a train for this afternoon. I can call you if you would want me to, or I could text you if you wouldn't want to be interrupted by the phone.

Oh, please. Assert yourself. It's not rude. Really.

I prefer arriving tomorrow but will look into this afternoon's train times. I will call or text you with my decision.

Not only do you come across as confident, you have also eliminated 21 extra words from the sentence.

I'm not saying to never use "would," "can," or "could," but when you do, double check and see if they can be left out.

And by the way, there's a difference between "can" and "will," with the former sounding hesitant unless we're using it solidly to say, "I am able to."

I have found this distinction especially helpful in asking questions and getting decent responses:

"Can you open the pickle jar?" implies, especially when I'm addressing a strapping, muscular male, that I doubt his ability to conquer the lid.

"Will you please open the pickle jar?" asks him to help the little lady out, without impugning in any way, shape, or form his strength and grip.

Must, Should, and Ought

There is a dreadful children's religious ditty that asseverates,

Everybody ought to go to Sunday School, Sunday School, Sunday School

The men and the women and the boys and the girls –

EVERYBODY ought to go to Sunday School.

If you have spent your lifetime trying to forget this tune, and I have slipped it back into the grooves of your brain, I apologize. If you have never heard the tune to this song, then I highly recommend that you NOT look it up and listen to it on YouTube.

You can't say I didn't give you fair warning.

So why is this song so repugnant?

The word "ought," – along with its cousins "should" and "must" – is one you want to watch using, because people – like your readers – not only do not like being told what to do, they also do not like being made to feel that somehow they are subordinate, inferior, and morally/intellectually/physically/emotionally substandard.

"Must," "should," and "ought" send subtle messages that the reader needs to (another form, two words this time) do or change something in his way of life. This message does not go over well with most people:

You should take the Commercial Exit. ("Take the Commercial Exit" works just fine).

Everybody ought to eat kohlrabi. (Do you seriously think this sentence encourages people to try a vegetable they don't know how to spell, much less cook?)

You must strip down to your underwear for a random airport TSA screening. ("Must" or not, there's no way to make this sentence palatable.)

Use these words sparingly, with discernment, and wisely.

Passive Construction -- a Powerful Tool

Anyone involved in any form of meaningful relationship knows that you don't get far with sentences like these:

You left the car windows open, and the cat jumped in and scratched up the seats.

We got charged a late fee on our credit card because you sent the payment in too late.

When you set the dish on the edge of the counter, I accidentally knocked it to the ground, and it broke.

Generally, the response to sentences like these isn't good, because the person on the receiving end feels -- understandably -- under attack and on the defensive. You don't need a doctorate in counseling to recognize that, when someone feels threatened or accused, he or she is highly unlikely to be sympathetic to your cause.

The good news is that there is a simple way of solving this problem, which basically involves not attacking people with the term, "You." Rather, we employ something that is called passive construction, and the best way to explain this is to show you how to use it in the sentences above:

The car window was left open, and the cat jumped in and scratched up the seats.

We got charged a late fee on our credit card because the payment was sent in too late.

I accidentally knocked the dish, which was set on the edge of the counter, to the ground, and it broke.

The key element of passive construction is that nobody really did the offending action, because it was done "by somebody" -- like this:

The car window was left open (by somebody), and . . .

We got charged . . . because the payment was sent in too late (by somebody).

I accidentally knocked the dish, which was set on the edge of the counter (by somebody), to the ground . . .

Of course, "somebody" is acutely aware of who he or she is, but because the accusatory note is removed from the statement, the defenses don't go up. And when the defenses don't go up, you and somebody are one step closer to reaching an accord on whatever it is you are talking about.

While this technique is invaluable in personal relationships, it works equally well in professional ones, especially when you are the underling being blamed by the manager for a problem that the manager, himself or herself, caused.

You will get nowhere, fast, if you shoot back with,

But you told me to call the client and cancel the order.

Anyone unwilling to take responsibility for his actions -- and frequently, people in power have difficulty admitting that they are wrong -- is probably not going to respond favorably, as in, "By golly I did!"

But if you reply,

I was told to call the client and cancel the order

you keep the option open to the person responsible to admit error, or not, but at least you're not forcing his hand.

This situation applies as well to a third party, say the boss of your manager who gets irritated because you called the client and canceled the order:

But he told me to call the client and cancel the order

sounds like tattling, whereas,

I was told to call the client and cancel the order

imparts information, releases you from responsibility (technically; the human tendency to find the lowest form on the food chain and make it the scapegoat still applies), and defuses the situation.

You'll notice that the passive construction consists of a form of To Be -- am, is, are, was, were -- as well as what we call the *past participle* form of a verb:

I am expected to arrive by six.

We have been told to park the car in this spot.

They were instructed to arrive by 3 p.m.

The passive construction also implies the term, "by somebody," after that past participle verb ("expected," "told," and "instructed," in the sentences above).

Does this work?

You bet it does. We humans are complex creatures, and the smallest things set us off. When you are faced with a delicate situation in which you want to clarify matters without throwing blame around, the passive construction is an aggressive weapon indeed.

Now, before we leave this chapter, a word of warning:

Any good thing can be overused. (That's in the passive construction, by the way -- I didn't want to set your back up by pointing my finger at you.)

In a future chapter, we will address terms like "moving forward with intention" as being a means of sounding pseudo intellectual without actual saying anything of import. The same people who use terms like these also fall naturally into the passive construction to describe just about everything, because they think it makes them sound more erudite:

With great intention and attention to authenticity, there is much to be said for multi-syllabic utterances of scholarly appearances that are not really expected to promulgate actual thought.

Overuse of passive construction, especially in conjunction with a lavish application of long, meaningless words, weakens your writing. Far from making you sound more intelligent, it makes you sound stuffy and stuck on yourself.

Use the passive construction wisely -- namely to avoid pointing the finger of blame in a delicate situation -- and the rest of the time, be forward and succinct.

THINGS WE DIDN'T WORRY ABOUT 150 YEARS AGO

As long as it's working, I really like indoor plumbing.

But when something goes wrong, like a mystery leak that drains the bank account as much as the water pipes, or a recalcitrant toilet, it's tempting to hearken back to the good, simple old days of chamber pots and chamber maids to empty them, providing, of course, that you're not a chamber maid.

Writing, like plumbing, has changed and evolved through the years, and some things, like the tendency to interrupt an exciting chase scene (on a horse, since that was the fastest thing around at the time), with five pages of philosophizing about mankind's relationship with tropical plants, are best left back in the 19th century.

Other aspects of modern writing, however, are convoluted and confusing, like indoor plumbing, and it's tempting to wish that we didn't have to worry about them.

Like this: if you're talking about a single generic person, do you refer to this person as a him, a her, a him/her, a they, or an it?

Is it this?

If an artist sells a painting for a good price, he is incandescently happy.

Or this?

If an artist sells a painting for a good price, he or she is incandescently happy.

Or this?

If an artist sells a painting for a good price, they are incandescently happy.

One hundred fifty years ago, it was the sentence behind Door #1. Now, it's . . . complicated.

Writing an e-mail; blogging; using "seminar-speak"; deciding between Mrs., Miss, and Ms. -- these are 21st century plumbing issues which we will touch upon in this section.

"Moving Forward with Intention" and Other Non-Communicative Phrases

Bigger is not better; multi-syllabic is not more intellectual than a short word; adding endings to innocuous utterances does not increase meaning.

Take the word "intention," as in – "We move forward with purposeful intention."

What is this saying?

Theoretically, it supports the idea of action, movement, purpose, and strength, but realistically, it says so in a weak, ineffective, unclear, vacillating manner.

Lately, "intention" joins a list of overused, under-meaningful words that launch straight out of upbeat seminars into people's lives, which they are instructed, authoritatively, to live "with intentionality."

Others are encouraged to seek "healthy authenticity" as they explore the "group dynamics" of a "purposeful community of decisively focused individuals."

While the people foisting these terms upon us collect fees for their seminars and classes that are, somehow, supposed to impel us to tap into the inner core of our vitality and vivacity of thought and movement, what they're really doing is obfuscating clear language with Corporate Group Speak – which at its base, really says nothing.

Think of words like money – use them wisely, use them well, avoid popular seminar-speak and "words of the day," and get the most meaning out of the least number of well chosen, expressive options.

That'd be awesome.

Gender Issues

Look at this sentence:

If a driver runs a red light, he may get a ticket.

Does anything about it bother you?

Some of you may answer "yes," others will shake your head, "no." For those who answer "yes," you're probably irritated by the use of "he" to refer to the driver, who could, it is true, be either a woman or a man.

"Not all drivers are men, you know. That's sexist."

I know. I hear you. I am a woman, after all, and I'm also a driver.

I am also a writer, and I watch as we transition from a male dominated society to an androgynous one, and in the process, try to determine what to do about a single person, whose gender is unidentified or neutral, wandering around in a sentence.

In the past the answer was this:

When you are talking about a singular person whose gender is unknown or unidentified, use the masculine pronoun he/him/his in referring to this person.

Hence, we have sentences like this:

A fool and his money are soon parted.

The average two-year-old almost instinctively knows that a tantrum will throw his parents into a panic.

How often does the CEO of a company stop to talk to his employees?

This is not to say that all fools, two-year-olds, and CEOs are men. We don't know who these people are – they are general, gender-neutral nouns, and we don't use the term "it" or "its" with people, as in,

A fool and its money are soon parted.

Some people solve this problem by replacing "they" or "them" for the "he" or "him," but keep the person they're talking about in the singular form. Like this:

A fool and their money are soon parted.

This one hurts, it really does. We have one fool, but several people's money, and what we wind up with is a lack of agreement.

After an artist completes a painting, they immediately start the next one.

The poor artist, alone in his studio, is suddenly inundated with company, messing around with his paintbrushes.

*After receiving their diploma, a teacher is eligi
look for a job.*

I wonder if "they" will help the teacher pay off the loans?

A chef is an artist, and their canvas is the kitchen.

Already too crowded, many kitchens are.

There is an intriguing theory that "they" is evolving into a term to express both the singular and the plural, in much the same way that the singular "you" and the plural "you" are spelled the same and differentiated through context.

While this is valid thinking, I'm not sure that we're ready to go there yet, but while I'm not a prophet, I'm guessing that that's where we will eventually end up.

Be aware, however, that if you use this technique, some people who are concerned about "agreement" -- meaning that a singular noun, like "the child," needs matching singular elements in the sentence: "The child eats his cake," as opposed to "The child eat their cake," or "The child eats their cake" -- can and will get upset.

If these people are instructors in a class you are taking, or editors of a publication for which you are writing, or managers who influence whether or not you will get a raise that year, you might want to ask them their policy on the matter and follow it.

Another band-aid fix is changing everything to plural, so that our one fool becomes many, and lots of people are losing on the exchange:

Fools and their money are soon parted.

While this is workable, it necessitates eliminating singular, gender neutral situations completely, which isn't a permanent solution. Several pages of referring to multiple people gets tiresome, not to mention starting to sound like profiling:

A French person pronounces his 'r's' differently from an English speaking person.

French people pronounce their 'r's' differently from English speaking people.

Maybe this doesn't bother you; if so, fill the room and pages with people. Just be aware that, at some point, you will craft a sentence that, within its context, begs to be in the singular, such as that fool, and his money.

Another solution, sort of a "fair is fair" resolution, is to replace the gender-neutral "he" with a gender-neutral "she," as in,

If a person wants to be a tugboat driver, she needs to practice driving a tugboat.

When the president of the United States walks in the room, she attracts attention.

Sorry. As a culture, we're just not ready for "she" as the gender-neutral option, and insisting upon it smacks of children in the car, arguing over who gets the front seat (although with the barrage of laws relegating children to back seats, that's not so much of an argument anymore). The question is begged, "How many years do we need to use 'she' as the gender-neutral noun in order to make things fair?"

Along the same lines, some people use "he" in one paragraph and "she," in another, vacillating back and forth between the two. As a reader, I find myself skimming back through the paragraphs, ensuring that the writer truly alternated between the two, and didn't use "he" twice in succession, or "she, she, he, she, he." This is schizophrenic and distracting.

So, what's the solution?

"We must create a gender-neutral noun."

Yeah, like the way we created the title "Ms." I detest the title "Ms." I am always reminded of Mammy in the 1939 movie "Gone with the Wind," referring to "Miz Scarlett" and "Massa Rhett."

Barring some self-proclaimed magazine solving the problem, however, we stand at the cusp of tradition and wait as general usage and regular people grapple with the issue. In the meantime, choose your gender-neutral weapon (mine is to use "he") when you have a choice, and when you don't, adhere to the style guidelines of the institution for which you are writing. Remember, there is nothing wrong with approaching the professor/editor/manager and asking him/her (oh, that's another option, using he/she, him/her, his/her – which works once or twice, but grates when you employ it on a regular basis) what his/her preferences are.

And before you grumble that things should be easier than this, and there really oughta be a rule, ask yourself, "Who makes the rule?"

Do I Use Mrs., Miss, or Ms.?

Love this one, because no matter which option you choose, you will offend someone. But that's okay -- so many people are so sensitive about everything these days that you'll manage to get on their wrong side just by opening your mouth, or typing Mrs. instead of Ms.

Ms. is a created word, not an abbreviation of an existing word (like Mrs. for Mistress, or Mr. for Mister) of the late 20th century to eliminate the distinction between Miss (an unmarried woman) and Mrs. (a married woman), a distinction that proponents said was unnecessary and sexist, because we do not differentiate between a married and an unmarried man.

Fair enough, although I wish the creators had come up with something that sounds better than Mizzzz.

That being said, I like the title Mrs., because I am proud of my 30-plus year marriage to the Norwegian Artist, and I do define who I am by the fact that I am a married woman. So when someone calls me Mrs., I am not offended. I am not everybody, however.

Keeping in mind that you will manage to offend somebody no matter what you do, the easiest way to get around this dilemma is as follows:

1) **Do not use the term Miss**, unless you're speaking to a 10-year-old girl. Use Ms.

2) **If you are writing to a woman for business or professional reasons, use Ms.**

3) **If you are writing a woman in a personal capacity, consider her age in addition to her marital status.** If she is married and older than 65, you will likely not offend with Mrs. If she is married and under 35, you will likely not offend with Ms. If she is married and between the ages of 35 and 65, use what you know about her to make an educated guess. If you offend, oh well; tuck it mentally away for future reference.

4) **What if she's divorced, or a widow?** Again, if you are writing in a professional capacity, use Ms. If you are writing in a personal capacity, make that educated guess based upon what you know about her, and when in doubt, use Ms.

As far as whether or not you use a period after Mr., Mrs., and Ms., you will notice that I do. Because Ms. is a created word and not a true abbreviation, the period is technically extra, extra optional, and actually not necessary, so people frequently write

Dear Mr. and Ms Jones

with the period after Mr. and not after Ms. While this is technically correct, it is also irritating, because it doesn't look consistent.

Whether you use a period or not, be consistent. Standard American English has traditionally called for the period after Mr. and Mrs. (whereas British

English has not) but people are increasingly dropping it, whether because of the non-period option after Ms., the general dumbing down of our collective consciousness, or a desire to get rid of superfluous punctuation. If you work someplace that uses a style book, consult that book for guidance; otherwise, be aware that in American English, using the period after the title, even Ms., is still common practice.

Online Writing and Key Words (Search Engine Optimization)

Several times I have run across online posts in which the commenting writer crows, "My article made it to Google's first page!" and then accompanies the announcement with a link to the article. The general message is that, due to a cleverly successful use of key words – the same word, repeated several times within the body of the article and/or its title -- the writer has driven traffic to his site.

Obviously, when I hit the link, I go straight to the article, but what I want to know is, if I type in the title of your article or the key words you have splattered all throughout, will you still show up on page 1?

Not always.

When I type in the key words (these are generally easy to find because 1) they are repeated to the point of nausea and 2) they are often underscored with links), there's no guarantee I'll get the promised article. If, however, the key words are unusual – "pink rhinoceros," say, or "beer syrup" – the article frequently appears, somewhere in the first three pages.

Also, when I type in the title, word for word, I generally do find the article, but take into consideration what some of these titles look like:

Green Zebras in Washtucna, WA, Stampede through Main Street

Banana Trees in Northern Greenland Are Fun and Easy to Grow

Make a Million Selling Chocolate Cupcakes!

If you combine the term Washtucna (population 212) with green zebras, it's highly likely that your article will make a successful page showing on Google. But how likely is it that anyone will type those three words together in the first place?

And so we come to key words and Search Engine Optimization, encapsulated by the concept that, if you use the same ordinary words over and over and over and over and over and over and over in the body of your story, or if you incorporate highly unusual words enough times ("exacerbate" or "samovar," for example), then you will catapult to the top of the search engines and be one of the first articles that people will find when they type in these terms.

Maybe, maybe not. It's when we think we're being most clever that we tend to get in the most trouble. And as intelligent as you are, if you've thought of this, how many other people – including the good folks at Google – have figured this out as well?

But let's say that it works, and people have found your article and landed on your page. This is an example of what they may be reading once they get there:

Happy people smile all the time because they're happy and a lot of people are happy because they're tapping into a powerful new concept that promotes power and energy in a positive happy way. The power of this happy concept is that it is simple and direct at the same time that it is profound and unusual according to many researchers in the matter of happiness and how it coordinates with power and contentment in people's lives, both happy and unhappy ones. You too can add to the happiness level of your life in a powerful profound yet simple way and the best way to start is by looking through the many options available on this website.

If you could make it through this sludge, would you be happy about it?

I'm not. I'm irritated at the lack of content, and rather than look around on the site while I'm there anyway, I leave quickly, because there is nothing that this person could say that would interest me.

Maybe I'm an anomaly, and maybe this technique works, but it isn't quality writing – and if you're out to actually say something worth saying, and you possess a modicum of respect for your readers, then you will avoid writing this way.

"Well, I'll just slip a word in three times or so, like 'croissant,' and fit it into the story in such a way that it won't stick out."

While it is possible to use a word repeatedly without seeming obvious about it, other times, an educated reader's first thought is, "Can't this person find a thesaurus?"

Bottom line: if quality of content and expression is your goal, don't worry about key words. If, however, you want to play around with them and try to increase traffic to your site, then do so carefully, recognizing that any compromises you make will compromise the quality of prose as well. What could have been superlative – writing wise – will now be, at best, pretty good.

Just don't get so far into key words that they accomplish one part of your goal – driving traffic to your site – while sacrificing what is hopefully the second part – writing something worth reading.

Online Writing – Simple Graphic Design Ideas

While we're on the topic of blogging and online writing, let's talk about some easy things that you can do – layout wise – to make your writing easier for the reader to read.

First and foremost, break up your text with paragraphs, which I address in the chapter, "Paragraphs Matter." Whether your writing is on paper or on screen, a dense block of it – unmitigated by white space – is easy to get lost in. Unless what you're saying is amazingly compelling or promises to turn the reader into a millionaire within the next five sentences, you will lose people's interest as they lose their place in the middle of that dense block.

Second, with the array of fonts available through websites and blogging platforms, there is no reason to use something that looks like it was typed on your grandfather's 1945 manual typewriter. Choose something simple and uncomplicated, and while you're at it, ensure that the size is at least 12 point. Many readers do not know how to enlarge text on their screen, nor do they have the interest in learning how to do so. Do not drive people away because of something so basic as the print being hard to read.

And speaking of being hard to read, while white or cream text on a dark background looks really cool, it's . . . hard to read.

Remember, the key purpose of all this "stuff" – spelling, grammar, punctuation, word choice, and graphic design – is to make your words and thought accessible to the reader.

Many online writers, for some obscure reason I cannot fathom, dispense with capitalization, something I addressed in the earlier chapter on General Rules of Capitalization. While online writing is more relaxed, it is not buck naked, and in rejoicing over your freedom of constraint, please control yourself. Capitalization and punctuation are there for a reason, one of which is, yes, because we've always done it that way, or at least done it that way for a long time.

But the primary reason behind capitalization and punctuation is that they standardize the text and make it easier to read, so that you can achieve your primary directive:

You have something important to say. Make sure that nothing gets in the way of people being able to read, and understand, the important things that you are saying.

Blogging

When I first started my lifestyle blog, This Woman Writes (www.thiswomanwrites.com), one of my daughters read it over and commented:

"This isn't blogging. Blogging is supposed to be random thoughts written without attention to punctuation or even to how the sentences are constructed. This is too organized and correct."

First of all, she didn't say it this coherently; she sort of, verbally blogged it.

Secondly, there is no Blogging Police. While initially, many people blogged in a stream-of-consciousness format, people like me came along and did it our way, to the point that now, blogging pretty much means writing, online.

This writing can be alternative news, political commentary, short fiction, informational articles, poetry, or essays like mine – it's all blogging, and the word has come to encompass so much that it's well on its way to meaning nothing at all.

And because blogging is open to everyone, its quality encompasses everything from absolutely amazing to insidiously insipid. As with anything – conventional media, movies, books (self-published or not), magazines – don't believe everything you read. Just because it's in print, doesn't mean it's true.

And if you blog, make a difference. You can start making this difference by writing well and coherently. Sure, you can churn out stream-of-consciousness, and if your reader base likes that, keep it up; but you can also plan out what you're going to say, self-edit as you write and even after you publish, and present clean, clear copy that engages your reader. Find what works for you and explore it.

Whether your readership consists of only your mother or encompasses a mob, the primary directive -- of clearly communicating your message -- applies.

The more you write, the better you get at it, and blogging is a great way to get more writing in. Just keep in mind that anything in cyberspace is pretty much permanent, so even though it takes the mere click of a keyboard key to get your thoughts launched, it takes far, far more than that to get them irrevocably erased. That's why there are "Draft" and "Publish" options on blogging platforms.

How to Write a Decent E-mail

Years ago, we worried about writing business letters. Nowadays, many of those business letters are in e-mail form, but in the process of switching from paper to screen, we have forgotten, or not paid attention to, the same letter-writing techniques that worked so successfully when we used a typewriter.

Because e-mails are instantaneous, we tend to spend about that much time on them, and it shows:

Got your message.

Will get on it.

Can you imagine sending a letter like that through the mail? Probably not, because it wouldn't be worth the price of the envelope or the stamp.

"But I know this person," you say. "I don't have to be formal."

True. But it would be nice if you would be a bit more *informative*.

Hi, Bob.

I got your message and will get on the project today or tomorrow. I'll send you the results by early next week.

Barb

At the very least, we have eliminated the terseness of the original message, provided enough information that the reader doesn't have to piece together random memories of what we discussed three days ago, and we don't sound like a grunting Neanderthal. If we are in the process of "conversing" via e-mail, shooting messages back and forth as if we were instant messaging or texting, then we understandably drop the Dear Bob and Sincerely, Barb parts, but at any other time, think of e-mails as letters, and adopt some of the elements we use in successful letters:

1) **Start with a salutation** -- Dear Bob, Hi Jamie, Hello Grace -- these all work if we are on first name basis with our correspondents, and they are a friendly, positive way to begin a message. If we do not know our correspondents, or if we are on a more formal basis with them, then Dear Mr. Brown, Dear Ms. Anderson, Dear Dr. James, will work just fine.

But what happens if we don't know the names of the people to whom we are writing? Dear Sirs is a general term of yesteryear that has the potential to cause offense when the recipients are female and technically, and realistically, not "sirs." Dear Sir or Ma'am is an alternative, but it's surprising the number of women who are irretrievably offended by being called Ma'am or Madam, as if we are implying that they are old, old indeed (these are the same people who will shout the roof off over their heads if anyone addresses them as Dear Miss, because this implies that they are young, young indeed.) To a certain extent, we have the same difficulty we encounter with the generic "he," which I address in

Gender Issues, and because we are dealing with individual people and a society in transition, there is no universal answer.

To Whom It May Concern is a generic solution that has the beauty of being completely gender neutral, but the unfortunate disadvantage of being cold, impersonal, and one size fits all, implying that you are sending out the same mass e-mail to 100 different recipients, but if you absolutely can't find a contact name, it, or a similar phrase, is your major alternative.

Dear Director, Dear Art Appraiser, Dear Customer Service Representative, Dear Newspaper Editor, Dear English Professor -- at the very least, you can pin down the type of person to whom you are writing and customize the title.

Try, try, try to find an actual name, and I sincerely hope that it isn't Chris or Jordan or Taylor or Addison or some other androgynous moniker that could be either a Mr. or a Ms. -- but if it is, and you've come this far and found the name, see if you can find anything further to give you an indication of the person's gender. And if you can't, you can write, "Dear Addison Brown," which I assure you is far, far better than, "Dear Mr./Ms. Brown."

2) **Write in complete sentences**, as if you were writing a letter that you were sending through the mail.

3) **Divide your thoughts into paragraphs**, so that the recipient does not have to wade through chunks of black type.

4) **Use a normal font, preferably a common one**. The more common the font, the more likely it is that your recipient's e-mail program will recognize and use it. If you use an amazingly unique and gorgeous script, it may be translated into Courier font anyway, because your recipient's e-mail software doesn't recognize it, and if it does, then your recipient is not going to enjoy wading through Palmer's Gold Leafed Handwriting.

5) **If you are not on an informal basis with your recipient, do not write as if you were.** (See the chapter on Formal versus Informal Writing.) There is a tendency to consider e-mails as a cross between memos and notes.

6) **Keep your topics to a minimum**. The more different things you discuss, the more likely that one, or more of them, will be overlooked.

7) **If you do have a number of topics to address, number them for clarity and ease of understanding**.

8) **With 6 and 7 in mind, keep the e-mails short, especially if they are introductory ones**. Many people get a lot of e-mails, and they read through them quickly. If they open up your message and see it extending far, far away, they may skim or skip.

9) **Take time with your e-mails, as if they were letters that you were going to send through the mail**. Somehow, because we don't physically hold our e-mails and sign them, we feel as if they aren't real, and anything we says, goes. But they are real, and if your recipient wants, he can print them off and hold them in his hand as he reads and re-reads them. You want to make sure that what he reads, and re-reads, is something that reflects well upon you and your message.

10) **Read, re-read, edit, and re-edit your e-mails before you send them.** I have taken as long as 45 minutes to craft a two-paragraph missive, looking for just the right word here, the right term of phrase there. "I repeated that word twice in the same sentence," I realize, "and it sounds like it." In the same way that you practice an important speech before the mirror, you review, and re-review, an important message before you send it. As with anything, the more you write, the better you get at it; while in the beginning you may take a long time to say what you want the way you want to say it, you will improve, and speed up.

11) **Be aware that your personality comes through in your writing**. If you write tersely, you will be interpreted as a terse person. If you are wordy and rambling, you will come across as confused and scattered. If you want to come across as efficient, organized, intelligent, and professional, then take the necessary time to ensure that your writing sounds that way.

The beauty of writing is that, unlike speaking to another in person, you can edit yourself until you sound right. And the beauty of learning how to edit your writing is that it does spill over into your speaking. The more time you take to write carefully and clearly, the more you stop and think before you speak, or act.

12) Close your e-mail appropriately:

Thank you for your time and consideration,

or *Sincerely,*

or *Truly Yours,*

or *Warmest Regards.*

Happy Weekend! Chou! See Ya! Bests! or similar closures are best reserved for people with whom you are on an informal basis.

If you're not sure that you are on an informal or formal basis, assume it's the latter, because you are less likely to offend by being too polite than too familiar.

13) Review your e-mail address and get a new one if necessary. SmokinHotDaddy@freemail.com may sound cool in some circles, but definitely not in others. My e-mail is carolyn@stevehendersonfineart.com, and while it is definitely not funky, cool, or edgy, it is also not puerile, questionable, or immature. Little things make a difference.

14) **Don't forget the subject line**. Of course the last item I address is the first one to which you should attend -- the subject line of your e-mail that the recipient will view before opening. Don't leave it blank, and make it as informative as possible:

Getting Back to You with That Quote

Tuesday's Meeting

Art Submission

If you don't know the person and want to make sure that he or she doesn't skip over you, inject a little humor or imagination, but don't go overboard. A recent unsolicited message from an unknown person caught my eye with the subject line, "Send It?"

My natural tendency as a human being was to think, "I must know this person even though I don't recognize the name," and I read the message.

I write a lot of e-mails, and I can assure you that the most wonderful thing about e-mail writing is also its worst: e-mails are quick. You write 'em; you hit that button; they're in your recipient's inbox, which is a great thing, and a terrible one at the same time.

It is far, far too easy to receive a missive from someone that, as Spock would put it in the 2009 Star Trek movie, emotionally compromises you, and while you are in that emotionally compromised state, to fire back without, um, thinking.

But once that Send button is hit, the message is sent, and whatever damage it can cause is being done.

It is also easy to be misinterpreted by too quickly writing back:

So what's the problem with that?

Are you serious?

Aren't you being a little over sensitive here?

Once e-mails become conversations, there is the risk that we will fire back and forth at one another until we eventually hit upon someone's nerves. An artist told me once of an e-mail he wrote to a business, offering his art as an option for wall decor in a new franchise that was being built. Upon being told that his prices were higher than what the business could afford, he shot back,

Art isn't cheap. But the stuff you put on your walls is.

"What I said was true," he told me ruefully, "but I pretty much shot myself in the foot in ever dealing with this company. If I had taken time to think, maybe walked away from the message for the day and re-visited it the next, I would have written something along the lines of,

I understand the difficulty of dealing with budgets, but I would like to work with you on yours. If you

could give me some idea of the pricing parameters, I will come up with some options for your review.

"Maybe it wouldn't have made a difference in this case. But I would still have a contact for the future."

Stop. Breathe. Read. Re-read. Reflect. Edit. Re-edit.

The more important the e-mail, the more that is on the line with what you are asking and hoping to receive, the longer you spend on the project.

Just because it takes less than a second to send an e-mail, doesn't mean that you spend less than a second writing one.

How to Write a Thank You Note

"Thank You" never goes out of style, and whether you e-mail, text, or hand write your expression of gratitude is up to Emily Post's descendents to decide. What I want to discuss is how to make sure your Thank You means something to the person who gets it.

1) **As with the e-mail or any written communication, start with the salutation**: Dear Person Who Gave Me the Gift. If you're on informal terms, use their first name; if you're less well known to one another, use Mr., Mrs. or Ms. Using their first and last name, Dear John Brown, sounds stilted and form-letterish. We all know how we feel when we get a communication addressing us by our first and last name, or worse, by the first and last name of our dog.

2) **Personalize it**. Thank you notes are not novels, and they do not have to be especially long, but they need to be more than,

Thank you for the gift. Sincerely, Me.

Surely, you remember what they gave you? Identify the gift specifically enough so that they get the idea that you really do remember it:

Thank you for the lovely flower tea pot.

That's specific enough. Now, add some sugar to the tea by talking a bit more about the gift:

I use it every morning for my morning tea. It looks so pretty on the dining room table, and it really brightens my day.

That's all you really need to say, and you can close the missive anytime now.

If they gave you money, then give them an idea of what you might do with it:

Thank you so much for the $20. For a long time, I have wanted to buy myself a flower teapot, and I will use this to do so. And every time I make tea in this lovely pot, I will think of you.

3) **If you need the note to be longer and you can't think of anything else to say about the teapot,** start a new paragraph and add a few lines about the context in which you received the gift:

I appreciate your attending my wedding shower. It was good to catch up after so long of not seeing one another, and I wish we could have talked more.

or

It was wonderful to see you at the housewarming. I appreciate your driving from out of state to be a part of this special time in my life.

4) **Close the note with a Sincerely, Warmest Wishes, Best Regards, or, if you're really close, Love,**

5) **Get the note out in a timely manner**, and if you haven't done so because you haven't had time to buy note cards and stamps, then either make a point of buying note cards and stamps and getting the things done, or send e-mails, regardless of what Emily Post's descendents advise. But do say Thank You.

Do I Say "Him and Me" or "He and I"?

Of all grammar questions that people pose, this has got to be the top problem.

If you don't get it right, you sound like an idiot (so you think), but be encouraged -- people of all incomes and educational backgrounds get this one wrong. On our art website, www.SteveHendersonFineArt.com, a blog I wrote on this subject gets hit time after time again, with visitors arriving from universities, state and federal government offices, private businesses, newspapers (are you KIDDING?) and once, Homeland Security.

While it's not a matter of national safety whether you say "Him and me" or "He and I" -- it would be reassuring to know that our top level public servants know their English, and know it well.

Well, let's get to it:

When you are faced with "him and me" or "he and I" (or "he and me," "him and I") -- drop the guy, until only you are left. Like this:

Him and me went to the movies.

Drop "him," so that you have,

Me went to the movies.

Other than Tarzan or Conan the Barbarian, does anyone speak this way? No, we say, "I went to the movies."

So at the very least, you now know that, regardless of whether you say "him" or "he," you will use "I," not "me," in this sentence.

Now, temporarily drop the "I" and see what you have left:

Him went to the movies.

Conan again. Most English-speakers by the time they are four know that we say, "He went to the movies."

It's time to put it all together then:

He and I went to the movies.

Isn't this fun? Let's try another:

Her and I ate the entire chocolate cake.

Get rid of "her" --

I ate the entire chocolate cake.

Sure did. I love cake. Since the "I" is correct, let's keep that in the back of our mind and address "her" --

Her ate the entire chocolate cake.

That's so cute. It sounds like my three-year-old granddaughter. No, we don't use "her" in this case; we use "she," as in:

She ate the entire chocolate cake.

So, *She and I ate the entire chocolate cake.*

You can also say, "I and she ate the entire chocolate cake," but that sounds stilted. It is, however, correct, so if you say it, and someone tells you you're wrong, don't panic. You're fine. It's just that, when there's a choice of pronoun placement (that's what words like "her," "him," "me," "I," "she," "we," etc. are called), we put ourselves last. Not a bad philosophy of life, actually.

Let's try a different sentence:

This gift is for she and I.

Let "she" go for a minute and focus on "I" --

This gift is for I.

Nope.

This gift is for me.

Yup.

Now for "she" --

This gift is for she.

Nope.

This gift is for her.

Yup.

This gift is for her and me.

Correct.

That's it. There aren't many easy fixes in life, but this is one of them, and the basic premise behind it, remember, is this:

When you are faced with two, or more, pronouns in a sentence and you don't know which ones are correct, use each pronoun individually to discover which one is right, then put them all together again at the end.

Let's practice:

I don't know why he/him and they/them arrived so early.

> *I don't know why he arrived so early.*
>
> *I don't know why they arrived so early.*

I don't know why he and they arrived so early.

We/Us and they/them don't get along very well.

We don't get along very well.

They don't get along very well.

We and they don't get along very well.

Last one; let's make it interesting:

She/her, you/you, and I/me need to get together with he/him and they/them before Wednesday.

    She need(s) to get together. . . before Wednesday.

    You (only one choice, either way) *need to get together . . .*

    I need to get together . . .

She, you, and I need to get together with he/him and they/them before Wednesday.

    She, you, and I need to get together with him before Wednesday.

    She, you, and I need to get together with them before Wednesday.

She, you, and I need to get together with him and them before Wednesday.

(By the way, if you wonder about the "s" at the end of need in the "She need(s) to get together . . ." sentence, every so often you'll adjust the verb -- "need" in this case -- to fit the pronoun. The whole sentence is talking about a bunch of people, so we use "need," which is the plural form. When we only talk about one person, we temporarily use the singular form, "needs.")

Let me repeat the rule:

When you are faced with two, or more, pronouns in a sentence and you don't know which ones are correct, use each pronoun individually to discover which one is right, then put them all together again at the end.

Thank You

Thank you for purchasing *Grammar Despair*, and for joining me on this journey of language, words, and communication. I hope that I have answered some of your questions.

I know that I will not have answered all of them, because language is complicated, complex, and constantly changing, and -- as I have taken pains to point out throughout this book -- the only real rule is that all rules have exceptions.

Read a lot -- quality stuff -- and ask questions. Expect that this journey of yours -- of writing, and learning about writing, and understanding our language -- is a lifelong one, and each day you will walk further and learn more.

Never let anyone make you feel stupid because you don't know the answer to something. None of us is God, although some people seem to think that they are.

The next book is one on punctuation, and the best way to know when it comes out is to haunt the Steve Henderson Fine Art website (www.SteveHendersonfFineArt.com), where we have a section on books, and Like the Steve Henderson Fine Art Facebook page. You can also find me, personally, on my site, This Woman Writes (www.thiswomanwrites.com), where I regularly post my lifestyle column. (I published formerly under the name Middle Aged Plague, which is cute, witty, and not set up for 30 years from now, when I will no longer be middle aged).

Additionally, I have published two e-books accessible at Amazon.com, *Life Is a Gift* and *The Jane Austen Driving School*, compendiums of my lifestyle articles illustrated by Steve's paintings (which are available as affordable signed limited edition prints and open edition posters, by the way).

You can reach me, anytime, by the Contact page on the Steve Henderson Fine Art webpage. I would love to hear from you. I also slipped my e-mail address in one of the chapters of this book, and you are welcome to write me with questions, observations, comments and general chit chat.

In the meantime, enjoy the process of writing. You have something significant and important to say, and the only one who can say it is you.

Made in the USA
Lexington, KY
09 August 2016